THE GREAT OUTDOORS BOOK OF

ALLIGATORS

By DICK BOTHWELL
Cartoons by the Author

GREAT OUTDOORS PUBLISHING CO.

4747 TWENTY-EIGHTH STREET NORTH   ST. PETERSBURG, FLORIDA 33714

CONTENTS

About the Author

RICHARD BOTHWELL
(1917-1981)

DICK BOTHWELL, feature writer and cartoonist with the *St. Petersburg Times* for many years, spent most of his early life in Wyoming and South Dakota before migrating to Florida. Since alligators are notoriously scarce in the Wild West, his first contact with the Original Floridian created a lasting impression..

Like all new arrivals, the young man from the wide open spaces wanted to be near water—and thus his first home was beside St. Petersburg's largest lake, 327-acre Lake Maggiore. Like thousands of other lake dwellers who have moved to these strange new subtropical surroundings, Bothwell quickly discovered that he had four-footed neighbors with greenish-black hides, many teeth—and large appetites.

He also discovered that in years past, when the town was growing and the Lake Maggiore area was considered wilderness, local police had given the lake's 'gator population a flying start.

Every time an anguished citizen called up to report an alligator strolling about the lawn or blocking traffic on the sidewalk, the law would dutifully rope and tie up the saurian intruder. Then they'd cart him (or her) out to Lake Maggiore, untie him (or her) and throw the creature into the water.

Nature took its course. By 1952, it was estimated that the big lake held some 100 alligators, big and little—all hungry. As the population boom surrounded the lake with homes, food became available. Scraps from people who thought alligators were interesting, and ducks from people who didn't.

As a reporter and a resident, Bothwell became keenly interested in alligators, as did his neighbors, when an eight-foot specimen calmly waddled up on a lakeside lawn and gobbled a pet duck.

Residents demanded action, especially those with small children. And they were astonished to learn that Florida state law forbid the molesting of alligators.

Pistols and rifles were brandished; more incidents occurred. The city's police chief personally shot and killed a seven-foot specimen in a resident's back yard.

And newspaperman Bothwell, curious to know more about the nature of the mysterious beast that seems half fish, half animal, began to amass the store of information that has culminated in this book.

In his years with the *Times*, he wrote of many things—weather, treasure-hunters, Indian skeletons in burial mounds and the wild assortment of human beings who make Florida what it is. But never did he have a more interesting assignment than Mr. 'Gator. We think you'll agree.

International Standard Book No. 0-8200-0302-6
Library of Congress Catalog Card No. 62-52-731

BIBLIOGRAPHY

C. J. Hylander, Adventures with Reptiles; New York: Julian Messner, Inc. 1951; D. B. McKay, Pioneer Florida; Tampa: The Southern Publishing Co., 1958; E. A. McIlhenny, The Alligator's Life History; Boston: The Christopher Publishing House, 1955; James A. Oliver, The Natural History of North American Amphibians and Reptiles; Princeton, N. J.: D. Van Nostrand Co., Inc. 1955; Clifford H. Pope, The Reptile World; New York: Alfred A. Knopf, 1960; Karl P. Schmidt, and Robert F. Inger, Living Reptiles Of The World; New York: Hanover House, 1957; M. F. Vessel, and E. J. Harrington, Common Native Animals; San Francisco: Chandler Publishing Co.

PHOTO CREDITS

Ross Allen's Reptile Institute: Pages 9, 10, 12, 18, 19, 20, 21, 22, 25, 29, 30, 53, 69, 72, 77, 81. St. Augustine Alligator Farm: 25, 26, 30, 36, 38, 76, 80, 82. St. Petersburg Times: 3, 8, 13, 46, 47. National Cancer Institute: 27. Nature's Giant Fish Bowl: 35, 37, 66, 69, 73. Weekiwachee Springs: 45, 47, 68. Godwin's Gatorland: 60. Verne L. Farnsworth: 59. Musa Isle Indian Village: 66, 67. Everglades Wonder Gardens: 70. McClung's Snake Farm: 71, 75.

Printed in The United States of America
GREAT OUTDOORS PUBLISHING CO.

Foreword

THE ALLIGATOR, when full grown, is a very large and terrible creature, and of prodigious strength, activity and swiftness in the water. I have seen them 20 feet in length . . . Behold him rushing forth from the flags and reeds. His enormous body swells. His plaited tail brandished high, floats upon the lake. The waters like a cataract descend from his opening jaws. Clouds of smoke issue from his dilated nostrils . . .

* * *

Thus wrote William Bartram in 1791 after the Quaker naturalist had traveled alone through the Carolinas, Georgia, East and West Florida.

This early-day traveler through the southern wilds had one great advantage in reporting his solitary impressions of the alligator—none of his readers could prove he was wrong.

Hopped up as Bartram's awesome account may be, there seems little doubt that alligators did swarm over the Southland in olden times. They numbered in the millions — and were a far cry from today's mild-mannered saurian.

Another historian, Thomas Barbour, recorded that "early travelers feared them, for they apparently hunted in packs, and were fearless, really terrifying animals."

Since Bartram's smoke-breathing monster first burst upon the reading public, the alligator has enjoyed somewhat lurid fame as one of nature's most fascinating and fearsome creatures.

Few visitors leave Florida until they've had a look at its famous armored citizen either at an alligator farm, a roadside zoo or right out in his native surroundings.

There are many myths and rumors about the alligator. Such as: He looks sluggish—but he can outrun a race horse! Beware his tail; he lies in wait beside streams and knocks unwary cattle off their feet with one swipe of that mighty weapon! Wrinkled, isn't he? That's because they live to be hundreds of years old, of course.

Now, just what is the truth about this strange, submarine-shaped creature that looks like a throwback to the Age of Dinosaurs? Although there have been many articles on various phases of alligator lore, to our knowledge there has never been an attempt to assemble all such information.

That's the reason for this book. We believe you'll find it a fascinating visit with one of the strangest critters on the face of the earth. Come, meet Mister Alligator.

Acknowledgments

Sincere appreciation goes to the many individuals and organizations whose experience guided our search for the facts about the alligator. I wish to especially thank James T. Floyd, assistant in the State of Florida Game and Fresh Water Fish Commission, book dealer Charles Haslam of St. Petersburg, F. Charles Usina and W. I. Drysdale, Owen Godwin, Ross Allen, Bill and Lester Piper.

To John Hamlet, naturalist at Weekiwachee Springs, we are particularly indebted for what we believe to be one of the few accounts of 'gator mating habits ever in print.

A special thank-you goes to Dr. Robert F. Hutton, biologist in charge of the Florida State Board of Conservation's Marine Laboratory at St. Petersburg; and to Bob Pixton and the late Jim Philbin—who kindly shared years of 'gator savvy with this city slicker.

Other names we'd like to add to this acknowledgement include Warren F. Hamilton, superintendent of Everglades National Park; Ralph C. Curtis, manager of Wild Cargo importers and dealers, Edward Rodriguez, wholesaler and manufacturer of alligator products.

Also I wish to thank two gentlemen without whom, as the saying goes, this book would never have been written: One is Dan Baldwin, President, Times Publishing Co. and our boss. The other the late Rube Allyn, Great Outdoors Publishing Co. head and an old friend who said, some centuries ago, "Why don't you write a book about alligators?"

The 29 Kinds of Living Crocodilians

Species		Found	Adult Length
American Alligator	*Alligator mississipiensis*	S. E. U.S.A.	16 ft. 2 in.
Chinese Alligator	*Alligator sinensis*	East China	6½ ft.
Spectacled Caiman	*Caiman crocodilus crocodilus*	South America	7 ft.
Rio Apaporis Caiman	*Caiman crocodilus apaporiensis*	Colombia, S.A.	6 ft.
Brown Caiman	*Caiman crocodilus fuscus*	Colombia to Mexico	6 ft.
Jacare	*Caiman crocodilus yacare*	Paraguay, South America	7 ft.
Broad-nosed Caiman	*Caiman latirostris*	Brazil and Paraguay	7 ft.
Black Caiman	*Melanosuchus niger*	Amazon drainage, South America	12 ft.
Dwarf Caiman	*Paleosuchus palpebrosus*	Amazon and the Guianas	4 ft.
Smooth-fronted Caiman	*Paleosuchus trigonatus*	Amazon Drainage	5 ft.
American Crocodile	*Crocodylus acutus*	Florida, Central America, Mexico, West Indies	15 ft.
Orinoco Crocodile	*Crocodylus intermedius*	Orinoco River, S.A.	19 ft.
River Crocodile	*Crocodylus acutus lewyanus*	Colombia, S.A.	10 ft.
Sharp-nosed Crocodile	*Crocodylus cataphractus*	W. & Central Africa	8 ft.
Johnstone's Crocodile	*Crocodylus johnstonei*	North Australia	8 ft.
Morelet's Crocodile	*Crocodylus moreleti*	Yucatan to Guatemala	8 ft.
Nile Crocodile	*Crocodylus niloticus*	Africa and Israel	16 ft.
New Guinea Crocodile	*Crocodylus n. novae-guineae*	New Guinea	9 ft.
Mindoro Crocodile	*Crocodylus n. mindorensis*	Philippine Islands	8 ft.
Saltwater Crocodile	*Crocodylus porosus porsus*	Asia, Australia	25 ft.
Ceylonese Saltwater Crocodile	*Crocodylus porosus*	Minikana, Ceylon	12 ft.
Cuban Crocodile	*Crocodylus rhombifer*	Cuba and Isle Of Pines	10 ft.
Siamese Crocodile	*Crocodylus siamensis*	Borneo, Siam, Java	12 ft.
West African Dwarf	*Crocodile Osteolamus tetraspis tetraspis*	West Africa	6 ft.
Congo Dwarf Crocodile	*Osteolamus tetraspis osborni*	Africa	4 ft.
Mugger Crocodile	*Crocodylus palustris palustris*	India & Pakistan	13 ft.
Ceylonese Mugger	*Crocodylus palustris kimbula*	Ceylon	12 ft.
False Gavial	*Tomistoma schlegeli*	Malay Peninsula, Sumatra and Borneo	16 ft.
Gavial	*Gavialis gangeticus*	India	21 ft.

Since the days when knighthood was in flower, men have been fascinated — and challenged — by the idea of a dragon, the ultimate in dangerous wildlife. Perhaps this explains why today's crocodilians are interesting to us all.

The Modern Dragon

YOU MAY GET AN unexpected thrill if you happen to be driving into Florida anytime soon. For there in the middle of the highway, basking on the warm pavement and reluctant to move for such puny things as automobiles, may be a genuine, real live alligator.

Most people are content to pull over to the side of the road and admire the native from a safe distance. Foolish folks sometimes yell "shoo!"

This impresses the alligator not at all. He knows perfectly well that at 12:01 a.m., Sept. 2, 1961, a state-wide closed season protecting all alligators and crocodiles went into effect.

Looking at your first live alligator, you might wonder why. He isn't pretty; his face would stop the proverbial clock. And his assortment of teeth are enough to make him look strictly dangerous — especially when he yawns.

But take a closer look. This is big business you're observing, all wrapped up in that armored hide. When Florida's new state law was adopted to save this famous tourist lure from extinction, W. Thomas McBroom of Miami, member of the Florida Game Commission, made a comment that was most revealing. McBroom said that about $500,000 worth of illegal alligator hides were sold each year in Miami alone!

Under the old regulations, commercial hunters were allowed to take alligators of more than six feet in length, except for a closed season in the Everglades region and certain other South Florida counties.

But Florida is still a frontier state in many ways. And in the Everglades area, the backwoodsman's old attitude of "I'll kill what I want when I want" is still strong, law or no law.

Thus game wardens, few and far between, were fighting a losing battle in trying to protect the alligator — especially with hides selling at $2.50 a foot.

This was especially true in the lonely reaches of South Florida, says Bill Piper, conservationist of Bonita Springs, on the Tamiami Trail.

On the long, lonely roads, a carload of hide bootleggers could see another car coming for miles in either direction. It was a simple thing to dazzle a roadside 'gator with a spotlight, shoot him and stuff the body into the car trunk. And who was to say if a dead alligator had been taken in a county where it was legal — or across the line in a county where it was not?

In dry weather, when Everglades canals sank low, the receding waters revealed a sad sight — the carcasses of alligators shot, sunk and not recovered. And occasionally, you might see the body of a small 'gator float by, tail chopped off for the meat.

Now, perhaps, enforcement will be simpler, and the Florida alligator will get more of a toehold on the comeback trail. This latest legal move is part of a cycle, part of a collision between populations — alligators and humans.

The Modern Dragon

Since 1944, the alligator population has been growing by leaps and bounds. That was the year that a group of conservationists pointed out two things to the State Legislature:

1) In South Florida counties especially, 'gator-made water holes were essential to conservation of wildlife during the winter dry season.

2) The alligator was being wiped out by hunters, forced out by drainage programs.

Belatedly, a law was passed protecting the saurians during breeding season, and taking of specimens under six feet prohibited year-round. Naturally, the alligator clan began to flourish. But Florida's people population was growing steadily too. From 1950 to 1960 the U. S. Census revealed a fantastic continuing climb. From 2,735,-413 in 1950, to 4,951,560 in 1960 — from 20th to 10th largest state in the nation.

Since both alligators and people are lovers of fresh-water lakes and rivers, the growing populations collided head-on. Something had to give — and although the alligator was there first, he has no vote at all.

Thus for several years the Wildlife Officers have spent more and more time capturing and transporting alligators from new subdivisions to wilderness areas. Says James T. Floyd of the Commission's information and education division:

"This becomes more and more of a problem each year as the population of Florida continues to expand and homes are built in areas that yesterday were the home of the alligator.

"In general, the Wildlife Officers of the Game and Fresh Water Fish Commission will capture and move such alligators that become a nuisance.

"In certain Southern cities we have entered into a training program in which the Wildlife Officer teaches the city police how to capture an alligator and either transport it outside the area of human population or hold such alligator for the Wildlife Officer."

Complicating the situation is the fact that there are two strong schools of thought on the alligator. One holds that he is a mean, vicious monster which will eat anything in sight, including humans, and should be wiped off the face of the earth.

The other school declares stoutly that the alligator is actually mild-mannered, lovable and nice to have around. The alligator says nothing. All he knows is, he was here first.

This is why the files of Florida newspapers (under A for alligators) have become crammed with clippings beginning: "Residents of Lake Blank are up in arms today over an alligator in

Look out, here comes Henry! At the Nature Trail, Lake Maggiore Park, St. Petersburg, this 12-foot specimen is king. This is how he looks charging. He was captured in the city by Wildlife Officer Jim Philbin, when a mere stripling of 9 feet or so. Henry hasn't forgotten — several years after his capture, when Philbin came to visit, the big alligator charged his old nemesis!

the lake that is said to have devoured two dogs, a duck and a prize Persian cat in the past two weeks. . ." — or:

"Traffic was blocked for an hour at the intersection of James Boulevard and 31st Street last night by an eight-foot alligator that refused to yield the right of way.

"Police, summoned by motorists, cautiously eased a noose around his neck and after a short but violent struggle, were able to subdue the beast and lash him to a plank for transport to a wilder spot . . ."

Typical of such dramatic episodes was an incident that occured in a Miami Springs canal July 25th, 1961. Two boys, Butch Davey, 13, and Paul Becker, 12, were swimming about with their dog, a mongrel named Brownie who loved water. Suddenly an eight-foot alligator surfaced near the boys, and snatched the dog between his jaws.

The Modern Dragon

Big George, 14 feet 7 inches of giant alligator, charges his master, Ross Allen, owner of the Reptile Institute at Silver Springs, Fla. The alligator, no longer living, was thought to be the largest specimen in captivity. This remarkable photo was taken by Mrs. Allen, a capable photographer. (Note: This photo is unretouched, unfaked. Big George is not kidding! Years of experience have taught Allen exactly how close he can get to a charging 'gator.)

There was a mighty splashing. Youngsters watching from the bank called for help. Miami Springs police officer Danny Clark, who happened to be passing, ran to the bank.

Clark fired once at the alligator, which was trying to make off with the dog. The bullet hit the reptile in the eye. He rolled over, vanished beneath the water, losing his hold on the dog.

A moment later he surfaced and charged up the bank toward the officer; then weakened and fell back into the water, going under for good. The dog's body floated to the surface a little later.

Alligators have appeared in swimming pools, front yards, in drainage pipes and canals, with varying degrees of excitement.

Accounts of such appearances will continue to appear in Florida newspapers more and more frequently. For Florida has some 30,000 lakes, plus many rivers and creeks, innumerable water holes and ponds, all to the alligator's liking. Slowly but surely, man is moving into Gatorland. Slowly but surely, it's getting harder for wildlife officers to find a place to move Mr. 'Gator.

Over the past decade, the southeastern states have realized that the alligator is a valuable resource which should be protected—as indicated by the state laws listed on page 85.

But just having a closed season isn't enough. Poachers, motivated by the high prices paid for hides, continue to decimate the alligator population; and enforcement agencies simply don't have the manpower to control poaching.

Florida's 1970 Legislature took a step in the right direction, however. The first bills passed provided for forfeiture of gear, vehicles, boats and lines of poachers; declared that possession of lights and weapons in the presence of alligators at night was evidence of intent to poach, and prohibited sale of alligator products in Florida after July 1, 1971.

The Modern Dragon

In wrestling, always keep a firm grip on the alligator's biting department. Note: It is important not to run out of breath before the alligator does, nor to allow him to entangle you in bottom weeds as he whirls. Ross Allen does the demonstrating above.

BUT I WAS HERE FIRST!!

Encounters between alligators and people are increasing in Florida. Reason: newcomers want to enjoy the alligator's native element — fresh water lakes and rivers, over 30,000 of them in the state.

Man Versus Alligator

EVER SINCE SAINT GEORGE took his very sharp sword, went up to the dragon's cave and whacked off the latter's head, man has been fascinated by the idea of single-handed battle against any fearsome - looking beast. That's why most visitors to Florida will make sure to see that sight of sights, alligator wrestling. This is a tourist attraction that really became big business back in boom days, as a novelty act to end all novelty acts.

A 1926 pioneer in the nerve-tingling business of facing and subduing a full-grown alligator barehanded was one Henry Coppinger, Jr. of Miami. In the words of a writer of the day:

"He thrilled and chilled thousands of Miamians and winter visitors with his death-defying exhibitions . . . His performances are almost too harrowing to be true." Coppinger, a jut-jawed young man handsome enough to be a movie star, operated an alligator farm in Miami, thus never lacked for sparring partners.

He was one of the first to adopt the chilling custom of diving into the water to grapple with an alligator in the latter's native element. At regular intervals Coppinger would have a husky 10-foot saurian dumped into Venetian Pool at Coral Gables, or one of the Miami Beach pools. Then, in a canoe, he would approach, dive in and tackle the beast. Trouble was, nobody could tell much about what was going on underwater — except that Coppinger always came up with the animal's jaws closed, held tightly in his grip, and obviously the winner.

Another daredevil of the era, one Capt. Earl Montgomery, did the same stunt in 1934 at the Miami Biltmore Hotel's pool. His technique was to dive in behind the reptile and straddle his horny back. Then working his way up the furiously rolling alligator, the captain held the jaws shut with one hand, using a half nelson on the strong but short foreleg.

You may picture alligator wrestling as a bloodthirsty encounter — but it isn't. In most cases the alligator simply wishes the man would go away and let him sleep.

Man Versus Alligator

Formidable alligator jaws are held apart in this manner, with the heel of hand on upper jaw, lower jaw gripped by loose skin beneath front portion. Danger increases when saurian's skin and man's hands are wet, making a slip possible.

Before pop-eyed winter visitors, he eased the alligator onto a floating platform, belly up, and carefully straddled the head, still holding the jaws shut. Slowly the alligator's eyes glazed and closed; the tail ceased to lash, its legs went limp. It was completely "out" and to prove the fact, the captain opened wide the powerful jaws and displayed his victim's teeth.

Two points are appropriate here:

1) Alligator jaw strength is oddly distributed. Tests at Florida's St. Augustine Alligator Farm have shown that an adult 'gator has a jaw pressure of up to 1,000 pounds! However, the jaw-opening muscles are weak, can be held shut with one hand if the 'gator doesn't move.

2) The swamp dragon, although capable of terrific bursts of energy, tires rather quickly. Here again, if he didn't, obviously alligator wrestlers could never bring him to the surface before they had run out of a couple of minutes worth of breath. Nature didn't design the alligator to wres-

tle; biting is his specialty.

City slickers got a real thrill at the 1950 New York City Sportsman's Show, when Tuffy Truesdale, professional wrestler who had switched from people to 'gators, demonstrated the art on a tank platform.

The alligator has four points of leverage, like a man on his hands and knees, Tuffy explained. Take away two of these points, throw the saurian over and the battle is won—if you're careful to stay away from jaw and tail.

We've talked with two veteran alligator wrestlers who've never lost a bout—the late Al Zaebst, black-bearded big game hunter and Ross Allen, head of the famous Allen Reptile Institute at Silver Springs, Fla. Both grappled with alligators at various times for the benefit of movie cameramen.

Zaebst used to advise hopefuls to dive onto the big ones—say a nice 12-footer. Reason: It's far easier to cling to the back of the heavier,

Man Versus Alligator

more sluggish type than the eight or nine footers who are more active in their whirling. The alligator whirl, incidentally, is his best tactic. And it comes naturally since as soon as his teeth close on prey, he twists sideways in the water in an attempt to use leverage to tear the victim to bits.

Common trick of the alligator, Zaebst said, is to sink to the bottom and attempt to scrape off or drown his "rider". An alligator can stay below the surface 15 minutes—which is considerably better than a man can do!

Ross Allen not infrequently gets requests from would-be adventurers who want to have a go at a 'gator, with his advice. He recalls one such occasion. Allen was going up a quiet Florida river in a boat with an ambitious alligator hunter, when up ahead, his experienced eye spotted a big one sliding off the bank and into the water. The guest "hunter" hadn't seen it.

Knowing that the alligator had probably settled to the bottom, Allen halted the boat in the area. Informing his guest that he'd take a look for any possibles, he dove down, looked around, and there, sure enough, was the 'gator, a big 10-footer resting placidly on the river bottom.

Allen had his favorite tool, a noosed rope, with him. He eased forward facing the 'gator and very gently worked the loop down around the neck. Had he touched the brute, in all likelihood the latter would have been gone in a hurry. But the alligator is not a quick thinker; perhaps the touch of the rope only seemed to be the brushing of a twig or debris in the current.

Robert Allen, one of Ross' three sons who've grown up in the alligator handling business, demonstrates safest way to hold an angry alligator's mouth open. Most people will take his word for it.

At any rate, Allen recalls, the alligator lay motionless. He swam back to the boat, paying out the rope carefully. Back in, he handed one end of the rope to his tyro hunter and advised him that a good strong pull would probably get him a 'gator. The amateur promptly applied a "good strong pull" to the rope and the sleeping giant down below went into action, churning up the water and threatening to upset the boat itself with his powerful tail.

Aside from an occasional mean alligator, the saurians are not nearly as ferocious as they look, which of course is what keeps alligator wrestling going. It reminds you of the human wrestling racket, in which some mild-manned, good-natured farm boy who wouldn't hurt a fly is led after big money on the grunt-and-groan circuit, wearing a black mask and billed as the Mexican Terror.

Alligators wear a built-in ugly job, but they'd rather just sleep and eat. Of course, you can make 'em mad — and some wrestlers do this deliberately.

In the wild, however, especially in defense of his home sweet home, the alligator is nobody to fool with. The late Albert DeVane of Lake Placid, Fla., long a student of the outdoors and the alligator, once told of a couple of instances.

Some 30 years ago, he said, when workmen were clearing a canoe trail, "While working through a large hole or lagoon in water almost shoulder deep, an alligator popped up in front of them and disputed their encroachment of home and domain. Carroll Payne hit at him with his machete. The alligator whirled, went down and caught Carroll about the knee. He hollered 'Boys, I'm 'gator caught!' "

"Two fellow workmen grabbed him and started for the bank before he turned him loose. Carroll was carried to the hospital for treatment.

"Word spread quickly about the incident . . . some hunters came and killed a 12-foot alligator from the same hole.

"Doc Durrance, another Lake Placid man, was also 'gator-caught. Doc was a great hunter. Most people like fried chicken and cake, but to Doc alligator hunting was his first love and joy. He was good too. One day Doc found a large alligator who had a cave on Stearns Creek. He tried 'grunting him up' (a method of getting in the water and making a grunting noise to attract the 'gator) but had no luck.

"The alligator had recently been shot at by fire hunters, but he had recovered. After that he would never stand for a light. He would sink to the bottom and lay there.

"Doc then made an alligator hook, saying he would pull him out of his cave and get him yet. He hooked him all right and dragged him out to the edge of the cave into the water at the creek's edge.

"The alligator began turning over and over and got loose and went into a large hole in the creek.

Man Versus Alligator

From Stefan Lorant's The New World (Duell, Sloan & Pearce)

According to de Morgues, who studied Indian customs and folkways, they fought and killed the huge, aggressive alligators of their day, almost four centuries ago, by ramming a sharpened log down the beast's throat, as pictured. It is possible that the alligator's size was somewhat exaggerated; also note that the alligator snout and feet are drawn much thinner and sharper than is the case. In the background, braves dispatch a wounded 'gator with clubs and arrows.

Not to be outdone, Doc got into the water waist deep and began to prod for him.

"The alligator eased up to Durrance under water and grabbed him on the thigh and held fast. By fighting and sheer strength, Doc tore loose from the creature but not before he took his pants and a hunk of flesh.

"It was a very serious wound and was several months curing up. Did Doc stop hunting alligators? I'll say not."

* * * *

You might wonder, seeing Seminole Indians wrestle 'gators around at Miami's Musa Isle Indian Village, if the red man has always shown so little awe of the "terrible lizard." Some five hundred years ago or more, might it not be possible that the inhabitants of primitive Florida worshipped the alligator, even as the ancient Egyptians made a god of the crocodile?

It does not seem likely from what scanty evidence exists. The alligator appears on the wooden plaques of Key Marco Indians, who dwelt along the Gulf Coast in South Florida and were the most advanced artistically of all the early tribes. But nobody is shown bowing down to the saurian.

The alligator would have made a wonderful totem pole, but the only one ever found in Florida, dragged from the muck of the St. Johns River in 1955 and now exhibited in the Florida State Museum in Gainesville, is carved in the likeness of an owl.

Man Versus Alligator

Some of the earliest drawings of alligators in the Southeastern United States were done by French artist Jacques le Moyne de Morgues, who was with French Huguenots who sought to establish a colony at the mouth of the St. Johns River in Northeastern Florida in 1562. Above, Timiquan Indians smoke game for their winter storehouse. Note 'gator, top right.

It is not logical that the Indian should have deified the alligator, who evidently regarded the red man as a canape on legs. According to Stefan Lorant's *The New World*, which tells of the life of the Calusas in 1564, the Indians kept constant guard against the alligators, staying on watch in small huts. This lends some strength to historical reports that the huge, fearless early-day alligators hunted in packs.

Illustrations of Jacques le Moyne de Morgues, who accompanied a French expedition to Florida and went among the Indians to sketch their customs, are a striking feature of *The New World*. Two such illustrations, reproduced in this book, show the rugged red men of that day killing the alligator and smoking him for winter provisions.

Certainly the Indian respected his rugged neighbor, however. One of the famed chieftains of the Seminole Wars in Florida was named Alligator and was believed to have led the Dade Massacre.

There are several words for alligator in the Seminole tongue, of which there are two main branches. However the root word seems to be *alla-paw-taw*, which is found in various spellings such as *hal-pat-ter*.

Generally, the relations of the Southeastern Indians to the alligator might be compared to those of the Plains Indians to the buffalo, to a lesser degree. (No teepees were made of alligator skin!)

The Egyptians fed their crocodile god an unnatural mixture of roast meats and wine. The horny-hided deity hated it but he had no choice!

Crocodilia Family

THINK THE ALLIGATOR is ugly? You should meet some of his relations — meaner, bigger, and uglier by far, worshipped as gods, feared as devils, with a family tree that goes back to prehistoric times.

The family name is Crocodilia. It includes crocodiles, alligators, and off-shoots such as the caiman (or cayman) of Central and South America, the gavial (or gharial) of India and Malay.

A direct link with past ages turned up in 1940 when an enormous prehistoric crocodile skull was found in the Big Bend region of South Texas by The American Museum-Sinclair Expedition.

Broken sections of skull and jaw were painstakingly dug from rock and pieced together. Result, "Phobosuchus," who, when he roamed the earth, must have been a truly terrifying sight. Picture a crocodile over 45 feet long, with jaws three feet in length, studded with six-inch teeth! Embedded in the same rock were dinosaur bones, fellow countrymen of this great-great-great grandfather of Crocodilia.

These ancient saurians saw most of the huge cold-blooded reptiles perish, unable to adapt to the changes which saw warm, humid climates become temperate and then zonal by the Cenozoic era.

Except for their size, these giant crocodiles closely resembled today's specimens. By the end of the Cretaceous period, they had evolved into three groups found today: The broad-nosed alligators and caimans, the pointed-nosed true crocodiles and salt-water crocodiles, and the narrow-nosed gavials.

The crocodiles saw the dinosaurs rise, decline and vanish. These survivors of the Mesozoic era, oldest of all living reptiles, saw mammals develop and man come on the scene.

They've taken millions of years in their stride while countless other creatures vanished from the face of the earth. Perhaps this is why these baleful-looking, toothy reptiles are so interesting to man. Perhaps people instinctively feel that this is the only living souvenir of the fabulous age of dinosaurs!

In ancient times, crocodiles are first mentioned by the historian Pliny. The old Roman recorded that 36 of the reptiles were slaughtered by Coliseum gladiators in the days of Augustus—or perhaps it was the other way around.

Even as today's Florida visitors, Greek historian Herodotus found the brutes ugly yet fascinating. He wrote that the Egyptians regarded the Nile crocodile with mixed emotions:

"Among some of the Egyptians the crocodile is sacred, while others pursue him as an enemy. The inhabitants of Thebes and the shores of Lake Moeris regard him with veneration. Each person

The Crocodilia Family

The oldest reptiles of the modern world — that's the impressive title of the Crocodilia family. A giant crocodile some 45 feet long roamed the earth along with the dinosaurs, saw them vanish and man come on the scene. The crocodile of that era looked little different from today's specimen. Aside, of course, from the small matter of size.

has a tame crocodile; he puts pendants of glass and gold in its ear lids, and gives it a regular allowance of food daily. When it dies it is embalmed, and placed in the sacred repository. But the inhabitants of Elephantine eat the crocodile, not at all regarding it as sacred." Other practical Egyptians used the sacred one's horny hide as armor.

One cold-blooded deity was kept in a tank in the city of Crocodinopolis, carefully tended by priests and fed an unnatural diet of roasted meats, small cakes and mulled wine!

The unfortunate reptile would probably have traded its best gold earrings for just one small raw fish. Instead, some of the huskier priests regularly forced open its jaws while others stuffed in food and sluiced it down the god's gullet with wine.

Hundreds of mummified crocodiles have been found in the catacombs at Thebes, mute evidence of one of the world's strangest forms of worship.

Crocodile worship occured also in India, where the toothy reptile was once venerated by the Hindoos and other sects.

The Greeks had a word for the crocodilians; they were worshipped in Egypt; thus it is not surprising to find the family mentioned in the Bible itself by another name—leviathan. This was also the Hebrew name for sea monster.

But a Bible encyclopedia notes: "As described in Job: 41, it is evidently a crocodile . . . a large water animal whose exact nature is undetermined."

Peloubet's Bible Dictionary says: "In Job 41:1 and Psalms 74:14 the crocodile is without doubt the animal intended."

Sounds plausible. Listen to parts of Job 41:

"Canst thou draw out leviathan with an hook? Or his tongue with a cord which thou lettest down? Canst thou put an hook into his nose? Or bore his jaw through with a thorn? . . . Canst thou fill his skin with barbed irons? or his head with fish spears? . . . None is so fierce that dare stir him up: who then is able to stand before me?

"Who can open the doors of his face? His teeth are terrible round about. His scales are his pride, shut up together as with a close seal. One is so near to another, that no air can come be-

The Crocodilia Family

Cuban crocodile, quite rare. Note speckled appearance of hide.

tween them . . . his eyes are like the eyelids of the morning.

"Out of his mouth go burning lamps, and sparks of fire leap out . . . The sword of him that layeth at him cannot hold: the spear, the dart, nor the habergeon. He esteemeth iron as straw, and brass as rotten wood. Darts are counted as stubble: he laugheth at the shaking of a spear . . . Upon earth there is not his like, who is made without fear."

One can readily imagine how man, armed only with a sword or spear, might find it difficult to dent the horny hide of an attacking crocodile. But the bold Timiquan Indians who inhabited Florida some six centuries ago waged a running battle with equally bold alligators swarming over the land — and the Indians often won. Their method was simple but effective, according to early French explorers.

The braves laid hold of a large log which they had sharpened to a point, waited until the 'gator had opened wide "the doors of his face" then rammed the log down the large 'gator throat. Smoked, the alligator formed an important part of their winter rations.

In later times, English writer Edward Topsell paid his respects to the dangerous Nile croc, which attains a length of 16 feet, in "The Historie of Foure-Footed Beastes."

He commented, (as did Kipling in later years) on the crocodile's habit of sunning himself with jaws agape while a small, reckless member of the Plover family hopped about inside the cavernous mouth, picking food and parasites from between the conical teeth.

"When all is cleansed," wrote Topsell, "the ingratefull Crocodile endeavoureth suddainely to shut his choppes together upon the Bird, and to devour his friend." (Florida crocodiles do their own tooth-cleaning, if any. American Plovers are smart.)

Topsell offered perhaps the most impractical bit of Crocodilia lore ever: "The crocodile runneth away from man if he wink with his right eye."

Because he inhabits a larger territory, the crocodile is probably the best-known member of the family. He is found in Africa, Madagascar, Mexico, Central and South America, the West Indies, South Asia, the East Indies and Northern Australia.

In the United States, the American Crocodile once ranged over much of South Florida. Today, however, he is becoming much harder to find.

Says Warren F. Hamilton, superintendent of Everglades National Park:

"The American Crocodile is in the extreme northern limit of its range here in southern Florida and in consequence is rare. As suitable sandy

The Crocodilia Family

Dwarf Caiman. From Amazon Basin, this species averages 3½ feet in length.

beaches for nesting disappear under the press of population, they will become even rarer. Unfortunately too, there is the problem of thoughtless hunters.

"Their survival under existing conditions in the United States is quite problematical and certainly can be assured only through all-out protection.

"At present, most of the known crocodiles are near Lake Surprise along the north shore of Key Largo, in Madeira Bay." (Everglades City Chamber of Commerce says crocodiles can be found from Flamingo in the Everglades National Park to Tavernier and Jewfish Creek on the Florida Keys.)

The American Crocodile is widely distributed, however, from the mainland of Central America southward along the Pacific Coast to Ecuador, northward to Western Mexico: in Colombia, South America, and in the larger islands of the West Indies.

The alligator's distribution is a zoological puzzler, for he is found in only two places in the world — two places widely separated. One is China's Yangtzke Kiang River area; the other, the Southeastern United States, primarily Florida and Louisiana.

From Florida, the alligator ranges northeastward up the South Atlantic coast to Albemarle Sound, N. C., and westward to Louisiana and the lowlands of East Texas; he penetrates inland along the Mississippi Valley in Arkansas and along the Pearl River Valley into Mississippi. (See State Reports, Page 94.)

Fossil remains show that alligators of several species once existed in many parts of the United States and Canada, as well as South America and Europe.

Brown Caiman. Note comparatively short head, blunt snout.

The Crocodilia Family

Lean, mean, and aggressive! This excellent shot of an American Crocodile shows to advantage the creature's lithe muscular body and sharp teeth. While the alligator is said by some to smile, nobody ever accuses his cousin the 'croc' of this. Note the grim expression around the eye!

Why does the creature still exist in China, where teeming millions are short on food, where fine leather is valued? Probably Alligator Sinensis, as the scientists term him, owes his survival to his dwelling place over the centuries—flooded alluvial plain, uninhabitable by man but ideal for amphibians.

One interesting theory for the two widely-separated homes of the world's alligators is this: That ages ago, the 'gator, like man, crossed the famed Bering Straits land bridge from the Old World to the new. Nobody knows.

Biggest of all reptiles, the crocodilians represent far fewer species—just 25 groups, compared to hundreds in other families. Except for the American and Chinese alligators, all crocodilians are natives of the tropics.

Colombia, South America, with seven or eight species, is crocodilian world headquarters. In all, South America has nine kinds, Asia six, Africa four and Australia two.

Perhaps one reason the crocodile is so much more widely distributed than the 'gator is its readiness to travel through salt water — whereas the alligator prefers fresh water. In one case on record, a crocodile is believed to have traveled 600 miles by water from one island to another!

Two cases of sea-going alligators in this coun-

African Slender-Snouted Crocodile. Body bears distinctive striped markings.

The Crocodilia Family

try occured off Florida's West Coast in the Gulf of Mexico in September, 1957. On Sept. 3, Bus Herzog, captain of the fishing boat Gulfpride, and Bob Hice of Tampa, who had chartered the boat, were 25 miles off the Gulf Beaches near St. Petersburg when they spotted what first appeared to be a log.

Closer examination revealed an alligator, alive but very tired. Even so, after being gaffed, socked on the head with a baseball bat and shot twice with a .22 rifle, he still tried to chew up the boat.

Nine feet long, the dead 'gator weighed only about 125 pounds, indicating he had been at sea quite a while. Normally, a male of this length would weigh about 250 pounds or more.

Oddly enough, another 'gator was seen 14 days later, on Sept. 17, swimming in the Gulf on three separate occasions. Could it have been the first alligator's mate, seeking her lost spouse? This specimen was not captured. But it seems likely that both alligators, rather than seeking to conquer new worlds, were simply mixed up as to directions.

The Order Crocodilia includes the Family Crocodylidae: Crocodylus, Osteolaemus, Tomistoma, Alligator, Caiman, Melanosuchus, Paleosuchus, and the Family Gavialidae: Gavialis.

The Indian gavial is abundant in the Indus, Ganges and Brahmaputra Rivers, and reaches the coast of Burma.

Orinoco Crocodile. Averages 10-12 feet at maturity but record specimen was 23 feet. (Only other member of crocodilians to equal this length is the American Crocodile.)

American Crocodile. Claws of front feet show wide, distinct separation in contrast to those of the hind feet.

Fortunately, its diet is almost entirely fish, and it is not known to attack man although big enough to do so—record length is 21 feet 6 inches.

Historically, the alligator is probably the best-known member of Order Crocodilia because he is concentrated in heavily-populated areas. Then too, he bears a strong family resemblance to the bad actors of the clan.

Crocodilians are similar in that they are four-legged, have a long, muscular tail, a body covered with platelike, horny scales, a long bony snout and numerous conical teeth set in bony sockets. All reproduce by eggs; some make large nest mounds

The Crocodilia Family

Can you identify them? In this striking photo, the major difference is shape of the head. Left, the pointed snout of the crocodile; center, the gavial's even more slender nose, ideal for this fish-eater's food-getting; and right, the broad, blunt snout of the American Alligator. Note too the interesting variation in hides. The crocodile skin appears more warty and lumpy; the gavial hide seems to emphasize horizontal ridges while the crocodile skin pattern shows almost square "scutes."

which they guard, others simply bury the eggs and abandon them.

But they vary in size and disposition, ranging from the Congo Dwarf Crocodile and the Dwarf Caiman of the Amazon Basin, both averaging about three and a half feet, to such dragon-size species as the salt water crocodile of southern Asia, which averages 12-14 feet. (See table pg. 6 for record lengths.)

Of the crocodilians, two are rated as most dangerous man-eaters because of their great size, wide range and ferocity—the Nile crocodile and the salt water crocodile.

Around the tropic belt, Ceylon seems to be the area where the greatest loss of life occurs. Government records in one district show that 53 persons were devoured in 25 years. A British government report in 1910 said that the salt water crocodile attacked and killed 244 persons in British India during one year!

There are periodic attempts to control or reduce the numbers of these killers. Yet villagers relax their caution after an attack at the river's edge — and another incident occurs. It has been suggested that the natives of these lands view crocodile attacks in a fatalistic manner, feeling that occasionally, no matter what, the crocodile will claim another victim.

How dangerous is the alligator? See Page 28.

The beam of the night hunter's headlamp picked up the alligator eyes, two by two, ruby red above the surface of the black water. Then the boat eased closer and the hunter killed his quarry with a shot through the brain "pan" just behind the eyes, as the dazzled beast hesitated. Not always, however. Keen of hearing, the alligator submerges at a sound.

Alligator Crop

THERE WERE 18,735 alligators taken in season of 1959-60. But that figure is puny compared to "the good old days" when conservation was unknown. In frontier Florida it seemed impossible that the supply of alligators could ever run low.

In the early 1800's travelers on river boats enlivened trips by banging away at alligators which swarmed the waters in such incredible numbers that it seemed one could walk from shore to shore on their backs, in the classic manner of Br'er Rabbit!

The Civil War may have hastened the alligators downfall. Post-war shortage created a new demand for tough, high-quality alligator leather. This in turn ushered in an era of unrestricted slaughter. In 1891, the Florida Fish Commission reported that two and one-half million alligators had been killed in the state over a 10-year period!

Cocoa, Melbourne, Fort Pierce, Miami and Kissimmee were important centers for hide-trading. Records indicate that ten men at Cocoa took 2,500 skins in 1899-1900. One hunter took 800 skins in one year. Another, 42 in a single night. At Fort Pierce, 12 men took 4,000 skins in 1889. Three firms at Kissimmee handled 33,600 hides that same year.

Along with the hides came other benefits. Alligator eggs were eaten widely. "Marsh-bar," or steak from the alligator tail, even appeared on the menus of backwoods restaurants. (Said by some to taste like pork chops, the white, solid meat has only a faintly fishy flavor.)

But the hides were the cash crop. By 1902, it was estimated that in Florida and Louisiana, only a fifth of the gator population of 20 years before remained.

The country was unable to keep up with the demand for the handsome leather. In 1902, U.S. tanneries handled 280,000 hides, worth about $420,000. Of this number, 56 per cent came from Mexico and Central America; 22 percent from Louisiana, and the remaining 2 percent from other Gulf states.

The alligator hunter of 1891 considered himself lucky to average 60 cents a skin for his dangerous work. By 1902, prices had soared to an average of 90 cents per skin. Said a U.S. Bureau of Fisheries report;

"Prime hides five feet long, with no cuts, scale slips or other defects, are worth about 95 cents each in trade, when the hunter sells them at the country stores, and about $1.10 at the tanneries . . . those measuring seven feet are worth $1.55; six feet, $1.12; four feet, 52 cents, and three feet, 25 cents. Little demand exists for those under three feet in length."

The souvenir trade also flourished as dealers capitalized on the appeal of the swamp dragon. In 1891 Jacksonville, Fla., had 12 dealers in live and stuffed alligators. The previous year, 8,400 live specimens were sold! Young alligators under

Alligator Crop

12 inches brought 40 cents to $1. Three-footers sold for $3 to $5, and $2 per foot was charged for larger animals. An exceptionally large specimen might bring up to $300. Highly polished, the blunt "dragon teeth" sold at $1 to $2 a pound, about 450 pounds being sold in 1890. (It took up to 200 teeth to make a pound.)

And what about the alligator? Here is solid evidence that he is not nearly as fierce as some writers seek to picture him — for in all the reports of alligator hunting, we find little evidence of the hunter being hunted. On the contrary, the saurians fell prey to man by night and by day.

It was a spectacular scene, this steady decimation of the living fossil called alligator. At night, the nocturnal creature's eyes gave him away. From a distance, they glowed like two bright orange coals in the glare of a torch or bulls-eye lantern, as the alligator cruised along, head barely out of water.

Blinded by the light, the alligator paused as the boat eased closer; at close range, a shotgun blasted off the top of his head. A hook pole snagged the body as it sank. The carcass was piled on the nearest bank. The boat moved on as the restless beam of light picked up another pair of orange coals just above the black surface of the swamp, lake or river.

By day, gangs of hunters sought out alligator dens dug by the water. These were easy to spot, since they were usually marked by narrow winding trails leading to the hole, and a smooth spot in the weeds nearby where the gator "pulled out" to sun himself.

A slender iron rod was used to probe down through the sandy soil and stir up the resident (if at home.) Once movement was felt below, the 'gator hook, attached to a long pole, was worked down through the den's entrance. As soon as the aroused 'gator bit it or the 'gator's body was snagged, two or three men dragged him out to be smashed on the head with an axe or shot.

Then the skinners squatted and set to work, splitting the hide down each side of the back to make a side and bottom piece in a matter of minutes. The hide was then rubbed thoroughly with salt on the inside, rolled up and packed; the party moved on to the next hole.

In 1929, the best hides were bringing $1.90 each, 190,000 being handled. Five years later the price had risen to $3, and 120,000 hides were taken. By 1940, the price was $7 a hide and only 75,000 skins were taken.

So rapidly did this trend accelerate that just four years later, when the state finally began protecting the alligator during its breeding season, a seven-foot hide brought $21 — but only 7,000 hides were taken during open season. (World War II, of course, played a part in this swift decline.) The effects of legal protection were quickly evident.

It is the alligator's misfortune to be encased in some of the toughest, handsomest hide in the world. The Egyptians used it for war shields and armor. Today, we make everything from key cases to shoes from it.

Three years later, in 1947, 25,000 hides were brought in. Price per hide dropped to $13.30; the alligator had been saved from extinction and his value as a crop finally recognized. Much credit is due a group of Florida conservationists who, in the early 40's had convinced Florida legislators that the alligator was going the way of the buffalo.

Their basic argument: Subtropical Florida has two seasons, wet and dry, with 60 percent of its average 50 inches of rainfall coming in June, July, August and September.

When it is dry on the vast open ranges and saw grass areas of South Florida, where no natural permanent body of water exists, alligator holes may be the only source of year-round water for cattle, deer, bears, rabbits, quail, turkey, otters, raccoons, waterfowl or songbirds.

Then too, the alligator is a great eater of garfish, which in turn destroys many game fish. He also eats fish-eating turtles; moreover, his water holes allow survival of breeding fish.

The state law adopted in 1944 provided protection for alligators and crocodiles under six feet, allowed no hunting at all during breeding season.

But six years later, further legislation became necessary. An increasing flood of complaints about alligators seemed to support what O. E. Frye Jr., assistant director of the State Game and Fresh

Alligator Crop

Water Fish Commission, pointed out: That evidence seems to indicate that the swamp dragon is apt to become bold and aggressive, especially as he increases in size, when unmolested by humans. Under such conditions, Frye added, the alligator may attack dogs, livestock, humans and other animals without warning.

For this reason, the commission moved to crack down on the big ones. In 1950, annual open season on specimens over eight feet long was set from October 1 to February 1, hunters being required to secure a permit from the commission.

The ruling was adopted upon recommendation of the State Alligator Committee, eight recognized authorities and sportsmen who had devoted months to study of the problem.

Some conservationists felt this was too much — but they were consoled by evidence indicating the big ones (usually males) are not good breeders and may actually reduce the alligator population by their cannibalistic nature.

Years ago the writer visited a most unusual business in Tarpon Springs on Florida's West Coast: The Florida Tanning and Sponge Company, operated by the Giallourakis Brothers. When alligator hunting was legal, this had been a major processing point. Before it became illegal, here's what it was like:

Step inside the doorway and you find yourself looking at a fairly rare sight — an alligator hide tannery. There's a strong, not unpleasant odor of hides and tanning ingredients in the air. In front of you is a rack of drying hides, moist and limp, all sizes — from big ten-footers to smaller ones, a dull medium brown color.

'Gators, 'gators, and more 'gators! This is the scene overlooking one of the main pens at St. Augustine Alligator Farm. Only thing that stirs this gang to action is the arrival of food.

Alligator Crop

Further along is the vat room, a group of tanks surrounding a huge steadily turning drum full of some mysterious liquid: "That colors the skins," explains Nestor Giallourakis, who with his brother Frank operates this unusual business.

It seems that the gleaming alligator skin you see on luggage, belts and shoes doesn't naturally grow that way. "It takes from 60 to 75 days to run a skin completely through the tanning process," says Nestor. "It's more work because it's so tough. That's why it's expensive leather."

Just what goes on in the tanning tanks? That, like the beer brewer's formula or the recipe for Coca-Cola, is a well-guarded mystery: "Every tanner has his secrets," Nestor tells you.

Once scales have been removed and the hide made soft and pliable, the trimming machine goes to work. The operator feeds in the hide little by little, like a housewife operating a mangle, and the rough, uneven underside of the skin is smoothed off.

From the vat, Frank shows you a piece of 'gator hide, now colored a deep rich cordovan—the result of over two months' work. The alligator doesn't know it, but he's got a hide to be proud of!

But it is the South American alligator, the caiman, who is really big in the novelty trade and skin business.

An interesting comparison; in Florida, a major alligator producing state, a legal harvest of 18,735 'gators was made during the year 1959-60, using State Game and Fresh Water Fish Commission figures.

But over the same period, the startling total of 100,000 caimans was imported into the United States, estimates Ralph C. Curtis, manager of Wild Cargo, animal importers and dealers of Hollywood, Florida.

(Curtis' interest in wild life dates back to his childhood when his grandfather brought him a live baby 'gator at his home in Illinois. Later moving to St. Petersburg, he became familiar with Florida reptiles in the wild and began a career in the field.)

When Florida stopped the sale of live baby alligators in 1944, this once-thriving business naturally collapsed, Curtis recalls:

"In the early 1950's, animal exporters in South America noticed the great abundance of the baby South American alligators, properly known as caiman or cayman. Since there was already a demand, it did not take long for the exporters to realize the great sales potential these reptiles would have in Florida. Today, the caiman can be purchased all over the United States.

"Until 1959, the South American country of Colombia was the leading exporter of the caiman for the U.S. pet trade. At that time the governmen of Colombia placed a ban on the export of these reptiles.

For some years the St. Augustine Alligator Farm used to present an alligator-hide football to the winner of the annual Gator Bowl classic. Valued at $150, the balls were made by Wilson Sporting Goods Co. of Chicago. Here, looking over the finished product, are (left to right) Bruce Colwell, factory superintendent, and Ed Reutinger, director of Wilson's School, College and Military Promotion Department.

"The ban was placed not for actual reasons of conservation as was the case in the state of Florida, but to insure a larger and constant supply for the leather tanneries and producers of the 'stuffed' alligators that are exported from Colombia. The Colombian Government felt that protection of the local industry was needed since, in certain areas, a great many people are employed preparing these for souvenirs to be sold throughout the United States.

"Since 1959, new export sources have been developed in several countries such as British Guiana, Brazil and Peru.

"For years all caiman hunters have been concentrated in certain river areas of northern Colombia, and there has been some difficulty in training new hunters and interesting them in entering the new areas. For this reason caimans have been harder to obtain during the past couple of years."

The biggest import season is from late May through November, when eggs hatch in the jungles and millions of baby caimans come into the world. By winter, Curtis explains, the caimans have grown a few inches and scattered over a wide area, thus being harder to catch.

Alligator Crop

At the National Cancer Institute, Bethesda, Maryland, alligators are used in the study of red blood cell metabolism. Since alligators vary their metabolic rates according to changes in surrounding temperatures, these animals are very useful in metabolic research studies. They also have the advantage of being large enough to withstand repeated blood samplings. In this photograph, Dr. Martin Cline of the National Cancer Institute's Metabolism Service lifts an alligator from an aquarium prior to blood sampling.

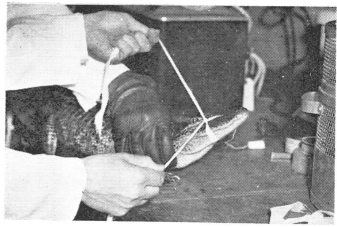

Step one in alligator research at the National Cancer Institute, Bethesda, Md., is—tie the jaws shut. This specimen, named Calvin, is big enough to be dangerous. Three years old, he weighs eight pounds. Raised in captivity, he was separated from his mate when he went into the science field. As a result, say Institute scientists, Calvin is depressed: "He used to come to the surface and eat, but now he just sits there."

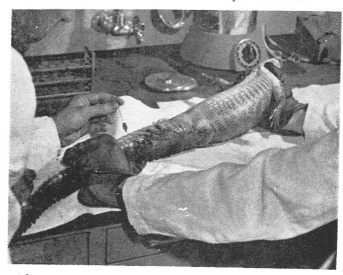

After injection of red blood cell labelling radioisotopes into the animal, blood samples are taken for study either from the heart or tail, as illustrated in this photograph.

Methods of taking caimans vary a great deal. Many are caught by chance, in fishing nets and seines. Hunters watch the eggs as they hatch and collect the young then; native hunters cruise the rivers at night in small boats and collect small ones by blinding them with a headlamp.

Shipped by air freight to the United States, the caiman goes to individuals in a sealed plastic bag which contains enough oxygen for a week, acts to retard dehydration of the creature.

Caiman cannot tolerate temperatures as low as those tolerated by the Florida 'gator; the South American reptile seems to do best at temperatures of 80-85 degrees. The caiman becomes dormant at temperatures below 70, at temperatures under 65 he will drown because of inability to swim or stay afloat.

Edward Rodriguez, Miami wholesale manufacturer of alligator bags and shoes, notes that the great demand for stuffed alligators is for those between 14 and 34 inches long. Caiman over four feet long, he adds, are extremely difficult to catch and have to be speared.

Caimans are cleaned, tanned and stuffed in South America; but the manufacture of products from the skin is a thriving industry in the United States, and in Miami particularly provides em-

ployment for the Cuban refugee colony and other Cuban residents of this country, Rodriguez says.

Handbags, wallets, key chain ornaments, key cases, cigarette lighters and cases, change purses, money clips, ashtrays, all are made by hand from the handsome caiman hide. (Shoes are made in South America.)

Thus the crocodilian continues to supply man, as he has from the days when his ancestors were worshiped as goods by the Egyptians, with leather for ornaments and practical use — and in some cases, with meat.

William Bartram, writing of his travels through Florida in 1791, declares that he once fought his way free of a ring of attacking alligators armed only with a club. It's hard to believe; but the old-timers were made of stern stuff.

How Dangerous Is He?

HEN IT COMES to the question of the alligator as a threat to man, you "pays your money and takes your choice."

Those who don't like him say he's mean, vicious and only too willing to sink his teeth into you. Those who do like him say he's a peaceable reptile who asks only to be let alone, but will fight when attacked like most any other creature.

Upon one point, however, there seems general agreement: An alligator is most likely to become bold and aggressive as he increases in size and is unmolested by humans. Under such conditions, says O. Earle Frye, assistant director of the Florida Game and Fresh Water Commission, the alligator may attack dogs, livestock and even humans.

It seems likely that alligators were much larger and more dangerous a century and a half ago, when Quaker naturalist William Bartram traveled alone through Florida wilds. Consider the following report he wrote of an experience he said

occurred while camping on the St. Johns River in 1791. Having pitched camp, he was setting out in his boat to catch a string of fish for supper:

"I furnished myself with a club for my defense, went on board and penetrating the first line of those (alligators) which surrounded my harbour, they gave way . . . but ere I had half-way reached the place, I was attacked on all sides, several endeavoring to upset the canoe.

"My situation now became precarious to the last degree: two very large ones attacked me closely, at the same instant, rushing up with their heads and part of their bodies above the water, roaring horribly and belching floods of water over me . . . . I applied my weapons so effectually about me, though at random, that I was so successful as to beat them off a little; when, finding that they desired to renew the battle, I made for shore, the only means left for my preservation."

A thrilling story. But viewed in a practical

How Dangerous Is He?

rather than a romantic manner, it doesn't stand up—unless William Bartram was one, the luckiest and two, the bravest adventurer of his time.

In the first place, a canoe is a tricky craft, which many people have trouble navigating even while sitting fairly still and paddling quietly. How in the world could it stay afloat under the assumed blows of enraged saurians each weighing possibly 400 pounds or more?

For another thing, what manner of wonderful weapon did Bartram use to make an impression on the armored skull of these early-day Floridians? He indicates he was armed only with a club. What a Samson he must have been!

Finally, what traveler (however hungry for a fish dinner) would deliberately shove off in a canoe toward a waiting line of hostile alligators?

Well, this was a century and a half ago. Nobody will ever know just how much of Bartram's story is true. But we do know that alligators have attacked humans. Probably one of the best-known attacks occurred Sept. 16, 1952.

A 10-year-old Coral Gables boy, Parker E. Stratt, with a girl companion, 9-year-old Jerry Gustafson, was fishing for minnows in a rock pit pool near their homes.

Suddenly, a seven-foot alligator came up from the depths, knocked the boy down with lashing tail and dragged the girl under water by her arm.

Many people might have run. But the young Cub Scout tried to save his friend. Fortunately, as the beast brought the half-unconscious girl to the surface, it lost its hold as it made a sudden twist,

The alligator doesn't look it, but he's amazingly flexible. Notice how this 12-foot specimen above has virtually turned into a doughnut to threaten Ross Allen with gaping jaws. Hunters say a 6-footer is hardest of all to handle, being most agile.

How Dangerous Is He?

the usual 'gator method of tearing large prey to pieces.

Braced against a tree root at the pool's edge, the boy leaned out over the water and pulled the girl out. Pushing her before him, he fought his way up the steep wall of the rockpit while the alligator waited below, jaws gaping.

Parker Stratt got Jerry to a doctor. Although her arm was broken and badly lacerated, it was saved.

On June 24 of that year, at the White House, President Harry Truman presented the Young America Medal For Bravery to a boy who truly deserved it.

In 1957, demands were heard for complete eradication of the alligator when, near Eau Gallie in Brevard County, Fla., a 9-year-old boy's body was mangled by 'gators. Conservationists said the child had been drowned before the 'gators touched him, but tempers ran high. The same situation developed in 1959 near Daytona Beach when another child's body was recovered from a alligator-infested swamp — but again, there was no proof that the child had not drowned first.

Near Largo, Fla., one hot August day in 1958 a road gang from the state prison camp in the area was clearing highway right-of-way when an

In the crystal clear waters of Silver Springs, Ross Allen demonstrates Rule No. 1 of all healthy alligator wrestlers—always approach your opponent from the rear.

Rule No. 2 in alligator wrestling underwater — once you've bull-dogged your alligator, get a good firm grip on his jaws, the better to hold them together.

A pretty visitor to the St. Augustine farm watches as one of the boarders scoots down the slide and splashes into the alligator pool. This isn't a "trick." The alligator is simply trying to get away from a handler at the rear of the slide who urges him onward. Alligators do not play with one another as do many young animals; for the 'gator, life is a serious business though he seems to smile about it.

How Dangerous Is He?

alligator lunged at one of the men from a thicket of high grass. A nearby guard shot the attacker. Alligator steak was the main course on the camp menu that night, and handsome belts and wallets were made from the skin.

In many cases, apparently a 'gator's attempt to get away — or to defend himself — is mistakenly called an "attack."

Some people are foolish about wild animals. For example, near Tampa in May, 1958, an over-bold citizen encountered a hitch-hiking alligator about 13 feet long and for some reason saw fit to grab the critter by the tail. The gentleman was fortunate to escape with only a few gashes on his right leg.

Such clashes were more frequent, of course, as the 'gator population increased following protection by law in 1944.

But although there have been many opportunities as people and alligators began to crowd each other in the Southeast, this writer has been unable to discover a single fatal attack on record. Moreover, wildlife officers agree that the alligator is not a menace unless disturbed or cornered.

Still, the argument continues — and will likely wax hotter as the 'gator crop flourishes in Florida.

In the summer of 1954, for instance, more than 60 alligators were captured around Tampa lakes alone!

Not many miles away in Bradenton, Wares Creek is a popular dwelling place for the armored Floridians, although the creek runs through the heart of town. In 1957 wildlife officers estimated there were around 200 alligators large and small dwelling in the creek.

(A few years earlier, a 13-foot specimen was taken from this creek, only to be returned later by Conservation men after irked creek residents signed a petition for the 'gator's come-back!)

Even outdoorsmen disagree about the alligator as a threat to man.

The late Al Zaebst, who figured he had probably trapped 1,000 alligators since he first came to Florida in 1921, always treated the swamp dragon with great respect. And he cited a case which he called an unprovoked attack:

In 1949, a woman was swimming in Weeki-wachee River on the West Coast of Florida when she was suddenly attacked by a large 'gator. The

Some people say that alligators are a threat to civilization and should be wiped out. Others feel the 'gator is lovable as a spotted pup. The fact is, he's neither.

beast seized her right arm, lost his hold, bit her left hand after flipping her over his back and then dove out of sight. The woman recovered after 23 stitches were taken in her arm.

The late Rube Allyn, Great Outdoors Publishing Co. head and St. Petersburg Times outdoors writer for many years, declared that the alligator was a female protecting her nest; Zaebst thought otherwise.

Certainly it is agreed that an attack is most likely to occur when the female is guarding her nest.

Wildlife officers who know 'gators best agree; the reptile is not a menace unless disturbed or cornered. Rube Allyn put it this way:

"An alligator really compares to the cow of our domestic animals. A human could jump in the same pond with a dozen alligators and never get a scratch.

"Alligators are retiring. However, if you were to attempt to chase a female away from her nest or corner a male and pretend violence, then, like any animal in the world, wild or human, they'd put up a fight."

But even Allyn, who considered himself one of the 'gator's best friends, admitted that there are "all kinds of animal personalities" including some alligators a bit on the mean side.

In the interests of safety, it seems best to treat alligators with all due respect and admire them from afar. That way, you won't be molesting this formidable citizen and he probably won't bother with you. Fair enough?

How Dangerous Is He?

"Behold him rushing forth from the flags and reeds. His enormous body swells. His plaited tail brandished high, floats upon the lake. The waters like a cataract descend from his opening jaws. Clouds of smoke issue from his dilated nostrils . . ."
—William Bartram, 1791

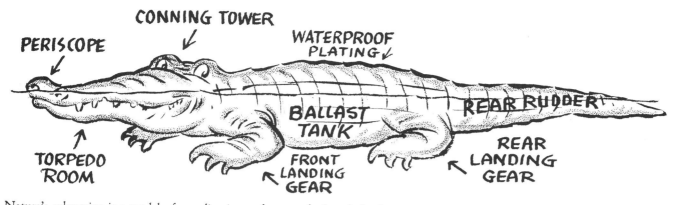

PERISCOPE · CONNING TOWER · WATERPROOF PLATING · TORPEDO ROOM · BALLAST TANK · FRONT LANDING GEAR · REAR LANDING GEAR · REAR RUDDER

Nature's submarine is a model of coordination and power, built of the best materials and heavily armed. No wonder it's lasted so long!

The Amazing Alligator Machine

ARLY SPANISH EXPLORERS of the New World called him the "Terrible Lizard." English settlers corrupted the name "el largato" (lizard) to alligator. Later, writers dubbed him "Living Fossil," "Reptilian Methuselah," and even less printable things. Naturalists just call him Alligator Mississipiensis.

But actually, he's the world's original skin diver, and one of nature's most fascinating pieces of machinery.

One of the most striking things about members of the crocodilia family is the way they can cruise on the surface of the water, almost like a submarine with only the necessary hunting radar showing — eyes, nostrils, ears at the same level, just out of the water.

Nature designed the alligator to look like a floating log just below the surface, with several knobs (the eyes and nostrils) projecting.

It is a thrilling experience to stand on the shores of a Florida lake on a quiet, pitch-dark night (when Mr. 'Gator is most apt to be out cruising around for a meal) and shine a strong flashlight out across the water's surface. If there are alligators in the lake, you'll see pairs of orange-red coals caught in the beam, moving slowly along like an automobile in the distance!

Those coals wink out in a hurry if you make a sound upon approaching; he can crash dive just fine, for he's perfectly equipped to do so.

Rangers at Everglades National Park tell you an interesting thing about those alligator eyes which reflect the light so brilliantly at night.

Young of both sexes and adult females reflect greenish yellow, but the eyes of adult males reflect ruby red, even from 400 or 500 feet. (The alligator shuts his eyelids to sleep even as you and I.)

Ross Allen, operator of the Reptile Institute at Silver Springs, Fla., has made an interesting discovery about these yellowish orbs with the black slitted pupil. The pupils are vertical and elliptical; if the head is tilted, the pupils stay vertical!

This "terrible lizard" is the world's original skin head. His tough hide is attached directly to the corrugated skull minus meat, minus lips of flesh which might serve as a mouth seal.

This wouldn't be practical. For one of the 'gator's basic maneuvers is to seize a large animal by the leg or snout when the latter is drinking, then pull the animal beneath the surface to drown it. The 'gator maintains his grip with jaws partially open; obviously he would drown too if he couldn't control his swallowing.

But his broad skull is engineered for breathing befitting such an amphibious creature. An air-passage, walled with bone, runs from the nostrils at the top of his snout to an opening behind his throat valve. A broad, thick tongue attached to the lower jaw can be raised to keep water out of his throat. The nostrils have valves; so do his keen ears, not noticeable but located just behind the eyes, under two skin flaps.

This is one reason that alligator hunting must be done quietly. The sound perception of man ranges from 15 to almost 15,000 cycles. Tests have shown the alligator can hear sounds from 50 to

The Amazing Alligator Machine

4,000 cycles — an ability unmatched by any other amphibian or reptile.

When the alligator dives, his nose, throat and ear valves are neatly closed like any good submariner's; then another ingenious piece of equipment comes into play — what you might call his goggles. Not only do his bulging eyes have upper and lower lids, they are equipped with a thin transparent membrane which protects the eyeball yet allows him to see under water. Clever people, these alligators!

Just how long can the 'gator hold his breath? Experiments have shown he can stay under water as long as five hours before drowning. Then why, you wonder, does an alligator wrestler dare to come to grips with the 'gator under water, in the latter's natural element?

The only logical explanation seems to be that he tires rapidly under such conditions, although capable of tremendous spurts of power. Certainly it is true that veteran wrestlers such as Ross Allen of Silver Springs, Florida, have gone down to tangle with the creature under water and brought him to the surface in two minutes or less. (Allen has accidentally drowned 'gators by staying under a bit too long.)

The alligator is not believed to be equipped with a particularly sharp sense of smell. His olfactory sense has been compared with the sense a shark uses in detecting blood in water at a great distance, however.

The alligator is no mean swimmer. He moves along at a good clip—about 12 knots—by using his powerful tail as a sort of sweep oar, while his stubby legs are tucked in alongside his cigar-shaped body. Some authorities believe he uses the hind legs as a sort of rudder.

One of the most remarkable bits of 'gator action ever filmed occurs in Walt Disney's "Prowlers of the Everglades," in which an underwater sequence shows alligators swimming along while swifter otters sport fearlessly nearby, secure in the knowledge of their greater speed.

The powerful animal is equipped with an impressive array of teeth — 70 to 80, although some writers yield to the urge to compare him with a piano and claim he has 88 ivories.

The teeth are all cone-shaped; he bites but doesn't chew, having no grinding surfaces. But here again, nature is ready; the alligator tears his prey into chunks, gulps it and a digestive system that could dissolve a locomotive goes to work.

He doesn't get a new set of teeth every two years, as sometimes supposed. Operators of the St. Augustine Farm say that there is no "period" whatever in dental shedding and replacement. Teeth come in as needed — humans would welcome such a supply!!

His built-in equipment makes old man alligator the world's first — and best — skindiver, except for one thing. For some peculiar reason, the alligator can't hold his breath as long as a man can while wrestling underwater.

The teeth are popular souvenirs, marketed commercially at $40 a pound.

At the Alligator Garden, San Antonio, Texas, Ross Allen once saw 11 eight-foot alligators that were toothless.

"They were raised," he said, "from babies by Catholic nuns and never developed teeth, I was told."

Few creatures have jaw pressure to compare with the 'gator. L. A. McIlhenny, in his classic volume, "Life Cycle of the Alligator," tells of an experiment in which an alligator bit a steel plate with such force that the long ninth tooth on either side of the creature's jaw was pushed up into and through the skull and had to be pulled out from the top with heavy pliers!

Neatly encasing all this spring-steel body is one of nature's toughest, finest hides — in a way, the animal's misfortune, since he provides such excellent leather that he was almost exterminated at one time in this country.

The Egyptians found this hide so tough it made excellent war shields. And some encyclopedias may even tell you that only a very powerful rifle can penetrate this armor.

The Amazing Alligator Machine

F. Charles Usina, co-owner of the St. Augustine Farm, found that bullets piercing the 'gator's body anywhere except in brain and nerve cells did not stop their movements. An alligator is tough enough to ignore a bullet hole — but even a .22-calibre bullet will penetrate his hide if well-aimed.

Incidentally, only the softer underbelly and side skin is sold to northern manufacturers for suitcases, handbags, shoes and belts. The horny "scutes," bony shields of the back, are too difficult to handle.

Usina has noted the extreme hardiness of the alligator, apparently almost impervious to pain. Effects of injury or sickness are hardly noticeable; sick alligators are rare. And an ailment that would kill a warm-blooded animal quickly may take a year to get the best of them, he says.

Alligators tend to be cannibalistic. On occasion, they will eat their own eggs, their young, even bite their own tails in the excitement of a mass brawl! Yet the loss of a portion of tail or even a leg doesn't seem to bother the swamp dragon much. At the St. Augustine Farm, one alligator whose top jaw had been torn away in a fight survived with only a lower jaw. He sunburned his tongue; he could hardly eat or breathe; but he lived for more than a year. (It is said that the alligator can live for two years without food.)

What does an alligator eat? You'll probably be surprised to know that insects make up a good part of his diet. Insects? Those tiny little things going down that huge maw? Seems incredible. Yet no less an authority than the U.S. Department of Agriculture says so — in Bulletin No. 147, The Habits and Economic Importance of Alligators, prepared in 1929 by R. Kellogg.

When you visit an alligator farm, you don't often see anybody walking. Reason, it's much nicer just to lie flat on the stomach, or crawl. But now and then when a bit more speed is needed, even a big alligator get up on his legs — like the one above at Homosassa Springs — and walks, or even runs. Alligators are capable of surprising bursts of speed for a short distance. (See Page 55, The Hunters.)

The Amazing Alligator Machine

Kellogg stated that stomach analyses of 149 'gators killed in Louisiana for the most part were as follows:

Crustaceans (crabs, crawfish, shrimps) made up 47.03 percent of the total food taken; insects, chiefly water beetles and leaf chafers, made up 20 percent; fishes, 14.04 percent; birds, 5 percent; mammals, 5.56 percent. Remainder of the diet consisted of a few reptiles, snails, and some vegetation such as woody tubers, burnt wood, etc.

The fish eaten included silversides, mullet, menhaden, killifish and alligator gar. (The alligator's appetite for "rough" fish is one of his greatest assets, some sportsmen say, arguing that every lake should have a few for this purpose.)

Birds found in the alligator stomachs included grebes, rails, and bitterns. Lest bird-lovers protest, rangers at Everglades National Park, Florida, have a good answer: For every water bird a big alligator eats in the 'Glades, he provides a feeding place for ten others. And the new crop of young birds each year easily replaces what they get.

This feeding place is the alligator pond in the open Everglades which is the reason he was protected by law there, even before the state's closed season went into effect in September, 1961.

As the water dries up in the 'Glades during the winter season, a big one digs into a low place still containing water, deepening it into a small pond. With his claws he tears soil and muck loose, washing it away with a current set up by movements of his powerful tail.

When the water table drops, the hole is made deeper; if bed rock is near the surface, he may be obliged to move to a better place.

Big alligators wander about, the rangers say, but will come back to the same little pond year after year and keep it from silting up.

These alligator holes are refuges in which fish can gather when the 'Glades go dry. There they provide a food supply for the wading birds —and water for many other forms of wildlife as well as cattle. Thus the alligator serves as a vital link in the teeming life scheme of the vast Everglades.

The crocodilian stomach entertains many items during the beast's lifetime. At a meeting of the London Zoological Society, a game warden of Tanganyika Territory, Africa, once exhibited contents of the stomach of a Salt Water Crocodile he had shot. They included three coiled wire armlets, eleven heavy brass arm rings, a necklace of glass beads, fourteen leg and arm bones from various animals, three spinal columns, several porcupine quills and 18 stones of various sizes!

The swallowing of stones to aid digestion, much as a chicken swallows gravel, is thought to be a trait of the crocodile — though not the alli-

Companionable comfort. Piled together like so many sticks of pliable cordwood, these captive alligators seem to get along just fine. Crocodiles, on the other hand, are never seen piled together this way; they're too quarrelsome. Notice that the alligator with head toward bottom of photo is leaner than companion whose foreleg rests on his back. Some alligators get jump on food as babies, never lose advantage — thus grow faster.

gator. Since the saurian gulps his food whole, it seems likely. Especially when we recall that dinosaurs did the same thing 70 million years ago, naturally on a larger scale. (Stones from the stomachs of both crocodile and dinosaur are on exhibit at Stanford University.)

This habit of random feeding seems to persist even in captivity.

In November, 1950, a Cincinnati Zoo crocodile named Mark Anthony was seen swallowing a Coke bottle. Since the 11-foot, 300-pound specimen was valued at $500, worried zoo officials decided to operate.

Mark Anthony was knocked out by a huge hypodermic, administered at the end of a 10-foot pole. He was strapped upside down upon a plank.

Zoo vet Carl A. Pleuger performed the first crocodectomy in history. He removed the bottle. Also five other broken bottles, three marbles, a .30-.30 calibre shell, a .38 calibre shell, a porcelain elephant and 39 stones. In the process, it was

The Amazing Alligator Machine

discovered that Mark was actually Cleopatra, a fact which got her name in the American Veterinary Medical Association Journal.

Lighter knots of pine have been found occasionally in alligator stomachs, although hunters doubt that they serve the purpose of stones. Could the pine, perhaps, act as catnip does for a cat in some manner? It is hard to believe that the alligator could mistake a pine knot for anything edible.

The alligator bellow is perhaps one of the most interesting parts of this amazing machine of the marshes and swamps. Just what does it sound like? Distant thunder — cows mooing — a heavy truck trying to get out of a mudhole? Everyone who's heard this powerful, explosive sound has his own idea.

Perhaps the best way to find out is to write Ross Allen's Reptile Institute at Silver Springs, Fla. For a nominal fee he'll send you a record on which you can hear the booming roar of the alligator, the high-pitched distress call of the baby 'gator—even the higher-pitched almost crow-like sound made by the crocodile. They may be stimulated to bellow by thunder, gunfire, blasting or the sound of a truck motor.

Probably the most novel experiment ever undertaken with an alligator occurred at the American Museum of Natural History in 1944, purely by chance.

Oscar the Alligator was an unknown, sulking in a large laboratory bathtub. An attendant accidentally "discovered" him. The man idly strummed some taut steel rods near the tub one morning and was startled to hear an answering roar!

Oscar was placed in a 17-foot tank and experiments began. It was found that each time the rods were strummed at 5 to 10-second intervals, Oscar would bellow. Plucked at 1-second intervals, he gave nothing but an irritated hiss.

It so happened that an orchestra was using the Museum auditorium for concerts at the time. Somebody had an inspiration. If Oscar roared for steel rods, what would happen if —?

A French horn seemed to come closest to the rod sound. A dubious musician was pressed into service. His serenade brought response "beyond belief."

When B flat was sounded, Oscar cut loose with "a sudden exhalation which produced a hoarse, moderately loud, deep note that suddenly increased tremendously in volume and rose in very sharp crescendo."

A cello player tried his luck. Once again Oscar showed his preference for B flat. It was plain that the instrument mattered not so long as the pitch was right.

At the American Museum of Natural History in 1944, an interesting fact about the alligator was discovered by chance. Of all the sounds in music B flat will make him roar like crazy!

An indication that the bellow, in the natural state, is a challenge as well as mating call came when a male alligator was put at the opposite end of the tank. Oscar ignored him. The French horn player sounded a call to arms (in B flat.)

Oscar promptly charged the intruder, bellowing his war cry.

At the St. Augustine Alligator Farm, a shotgun blast will set off a symphonic bellowing that fairly shakes the concrete buildings. During World War II, a Coast Guard firing range within earshot kept the alligators so stirred up that they bellowed incessantly for days on end and were worn to a frazzle.

Although the visitor to Florida may still hear the sound in 'gatorland during mating season, it is a faint echo of the by-gone days when countless thousands of bold alligators roamed the land. An early-day traveler declared:

"It (the bellowing) most resembles very heavy distant thunder, not only shaking the air and waters, but causing the earth to tremble; and when hundreds and thousands are roaring at the same time, you can scarcely be persuaded but that the whole globe is violently and dangerously agitated."

The Amazing Alligator Machine

This, then, is the amazing 'gator machine — perfectly adapted to his amphibious life, with partially-webbed feet to bear him over marshy ground when need be, speed enough to catch his dinner in the water, guile enough to trap the unwary land animal, plus a powerful, durable body and little sense of pain. No wonder he has lasted since the age of dinosaurs!

It is believed that a Nile Crocodile usually has about 10 pounds of stones in his stomach. An English scientist in April, 1962, offered one of the most remarkable explanations for this fact ever heard. The crocodile, he reasoned, is not properly balanced by nature, being top-heavy as well as tail-heavy. Therefore the critter gulps a bunch of rocks to serve as ballast!

It would be surprising to say the least to find that nature, after equipping the crocodilian so superbly in every other manner should have neglected to throw in proper balance. If this theory is correct, perhaps even the huge dinosaurs had a hard time keeping their feet while they reeled about, searching anxiously for some boulders to insure a steady gait.

Here is a perfect example of the manner in which this most curious of all beasts attracts odd theories and beliefs.

How fat can you get? In the case of the two bulging suitcases above, there's apparently almost no limit. These overstuffed, grinning specimens probably weigh almost twice what a wild alligator (who has to go out and grab his own grub) would weigh. Life on the farm is wonderful — when you're fed daily!

Novelist Tom Helm is perhaps the only man around who can tell you what it feels like to have an alligator for a bedfellow while camping out. Exciting, that's what!

Myths and Facts

IN A CORNER OF Everglades Wonder Gardens wildlife museum at Bonita Springs, Fla., on the Tamiami Trail, two huge white skulls sit in a corner showcase. They represent the big difference between the alligator and the crocodile.

On the crocodile's long, tapered snout, the enlarged fourth tooth in the lower jaw shows when the top jaw fits down, fitting neatly into a groove in the latter jaw. On the alligator skull, this lower tooth doesn't show when the jaws are closed. In fact, mostly upper teeth are seen when the 'gator smiles.

Although this point has been reprinted many times, few people remember it. In fact, a host of misconceptions exist concerning the alligator and the crocodile. The creatures are ideal for the tall tale spinner, for most folks have seen them only in the movies — which usually make the poor old alligator out to be a deadly killer.

What color is an alligator? Most people might say "green," because he's usually pictured that way. But actually, his base color is black, whereas a crocodile's base color is olive gray with dark bands and spots. A muddy alligator can look gray, too, which accounts for the frequent mistaking of alligator for crocodile by those not familiar with the two. The young are a bit more colorful.

A young 'gator's black paint job is tricked out with yellowish striping and spots. A young crocodile has rows of black spots on his gray hide, while a young spectacled caiman is greenish with dark spots and crossbands on body and tail. These amphibians are perfectly camouflaged by nature for their surroundings.

More lithe and active, the crocodile is generally agreed to be much more vicious than the 'gator. Rube Allyn, longtime Florida naturalist and outdoorsman, rated the crocodile as the tiger of the species, the alligator as the milk cow.

There's a definite difference. For example, at the St. Augustine (Fla.) Alligator Farm, it has been noted that alligators chomp down on food for the simple purpose of eating it. Crocodiles, however, seem to bite viciously for the pure pleasure of biting. They may chew into a piece of meat and then walk away from it.

One illusion about the crocodilia family goes back as far as the Greek historian Herodotus, who

Myths and Facts

"I said to my partner, 'Lige, that alligator's between my legs!'"

relayed a popular story heard to this day: That the crocodile opens its mouth via a hinged upper jaw, whereas the alligator's lower jaw is hinged to the skull in the conventional manner.

Watching an open-mouthed crocodile or alligator basking in the sun, the careless observer might easily think that the upper jaw was moveable. But in reality the brute simply raises his head and allows his jaw to drop. It is only the snake that has an upper jaw separately hinged to his skull, to permit swallowing of large-sized prey. Since a big alligator is capable of gulping a good-sized pig, let us be grateful his jaws don't open both ways!

One of the strangest true stories about alligators (in a state where alligator stories are common as sand) was told to us by Tom Helm, Dunedin, Fla., author and naturalist.

Some years ago Helm and a friend were on a camping trip and bedded down for the night in open country up in North Florida.

In the middle of the night, Helm woke up and sensed that all was not as it should be. He reached behind him with a hand and felt something like a large, cold suitcase.

On the other side of the "suitcase," Helm's chum was also aquiver. A single word of agreement and the two men exploded out of either side of their tent while an alligator who had innocently sought warmth took off with their canvas flapping about him!

"It was dark," says Helm, "and we were dancing barefoot around palmetto stubs — but that 'gator must have been a hundred feet long!"

Everyone has heard of another cold-blooded type, the snake, seeking a little warmth in a cowboy's blanket at night on the prairies — but an alligator makes an even worse bed-partner.

Up on Florida's West Coast on U.S. Highway 19, near New Port Richey, there stands a most unusual house of bright red and green. It belongs to R. F. Equevilley, descendant of French nobility and veteran outdoorsman in these parts. (His ability is underlined by a startling display of ten bear skulls on his living room wall.)

The old-timer once gave us a bit of alligator lore which will come in handy for anyone seeking the thrill of hunting the creature in the dark of a swamp:

"We were hunting 'gators one night," he grins. "I was standing in a pond, and I jabbed this 'gator with a pole. Then I felt him between my legs. I said to my partner, 'Lige, that 'gator's between my legs!' He said, 'What do you want me to do?' I said, 'Nothing, dammit! Be still!' Because if you touch a 'gator he'll bite you — but if he touches you, he won't. He went on through my legs. He was 12 feet long."

A veteran hunter of Homosassa, Fla., tells of a strange experience he swears is true. One night there was a full moon and he was easing through the swamp when he heard an unearthly chorus. Moving toward it, he came upon a clearing and there, upright on their haunches, were four big alligators, snouts raised to the sky, bellowing out a wild chorus to the moon!

Do 'gators have a place where they go to die when they grow old, such as the popular story of the elephants burying grounds? Could be. It is remarkable how few reports are made of alligators dead from natural causes.

How old do the crocodilians get to be? Here again, the tall story artists have made the sky the limit. In a Florida magazine published during the state's big boom of 1925-26, we find a writer seriously stating that "The alligator does not reach middle age until it has celebrated its 500th birth-

Myths and Facts

day . Alligators have lived to be more than 1,000 years old. It looks as though the reptile finally dies just in order to experience a new sensation."

Obviously nobody could have been around to record the birth of a 1,000-year-old alligator — except a 1,000-year-old (plus) man! But even today at various roadside zoos you'll find the sign, over the biggest, fattest 'gator, "100 years old." This is what a bad complexion will do for one.

Even a 500-year-old alligator would have been fair-sized when Columbus landed in the New World. No, the fact is that nobody knows just how long an alligator lives in natural surroundings.

The late Major Stanley S. Flower made a study indicating 56 years was tops for an American alligator in captivity; 50 years for a Chinese alligator, and 31 years for a marsh crocodile, all still alive at the time.

Size is no sure yardstick in determining age, either, although more studies have been made of the American alligator than any other member of the family.

E.A. McIlhenny, Louisiana naturalist, marked specimens and turned them loose, later re-capturing them for measurement. He found that the 8 or 9-inch baby which emerges from the egg grows fairly rapidly in nature when adequate food is available. Average length at two years of age was 40.7 inches; at four years, 62 inches; and six years 72 inches. During this year males seem to begin to outstrip females in growth until at the age of 10 the males are about two feet longer (averaging 9 feet 2 inches) and about two and a quarter times as heavy, weighing around 250 pounds.

McIlhenny also found that both sexes attain sexual maturity at about six years. After this point, growth may be so slow that it is not known if it stops completely or continues at a very slow rate. The latter seems more likely.

The female alligator seldom measures over nine feet long, or weighs more than 160 pounds. By contrast, a male 11-12 feet long will weigh 450 to 550 pounds.

Ross Allen and Wilfred T. Neill, Reptile Institute naturalists, observe that captive alligators, often kept under improper conditions, may grow very little. This fact, they believe, may mislead people into supposing that big alligators must be very, very old.

If you wanted to start a myth about a ghost alligator, the place to do it would be around the Palenque River of Colombia, South America. There albino specimens have been reported occasionally. Ross Allen's Reptile Institute at Silver Springs has a grayish specimen—not albino, says Allen, but a blond.

This strange illustration is probably the most unusual drawing of a crocodilian ever made. The lady seems to be perfectly calm about a double hazard—falling on the ice and her odd skating companion. From the drawings of Heinrich Kley, Dover Publications, Inc., 180 Varick Street, New York 14, New York.

The St. Augustine Alligator Farm boasts a *red* alligator, believed to be the only one in existence. It was believed by the late G. Kingsley Noble, of the American Museum of Natural History, to be due to erythrism, a condition in which black pigment cells do not oxidize, but remain red, the color of the alligator fetus in the egg before hatching.

Dr. William Etkin, a colleague of Dr. Noble, suggests that amphibians are somewhat like chameleons, with pituitary conditions determining coloration. If so, then St. Augustine's red alligator is like a huge chameleon whose color spectrum stopped on red.

One of the oddest cases involving alligators took place in January, 1957, at Tavares, Florida. One Albert M. Trull of Bushnell had been convicted and fined $250 in Sumter County Court for having a number of undersized alligator hides in his possession, a violation of state law.

He appealed to the court on the grounds that the alligator is neither reptile nor amphibian and that therefore game wardens had no authority to arrest him!

Circuit Judge Truman G. Futch took several weeks to study the 'gator family tree. Finally, he ruled Trull innocent because the State Game and Fresh Water Fish Commission had failed to file

Myths and Facts

copies of its alligator regulations with each state attorney's office and county court in Florida.

An unusual killing occured in May, 1957, when a dairy farm worker near Parrish, Florida, was tossing hay in a hayloft when he heard cows stampeding below.

He climbed down to see what was wrong and almost walked into the jaws of a hungry, 7-foot, 300-pound alligator seeking to grab a calf. It was probably the only time in history when a pitchfork was used to kill an alligator.

Don't think the 'gator is just a mere sun-worshipper on the ugly side, however. He's actually making quite a contribution to national defense and to science!

We learned this accidentally while looking into the operation of C. C. McClung's Snake Farm at LaPlace, La. He mentioned that for some unknown reason, three national agencies have requested live alligators from him from time to time. Here was a mystery.

What in the world could the U.S. Army Chemical Center at Maryland have done with 25 alligators over the past six years? We still don't know for sure. Here's the answer from Floyd Brinkley, technical liaison officer:

"They (the alligators) have been used for basic studies in respiration and metabolism connected with Chemical Corps research. The work is of a classified nature; however, it may be said that the alligator served to improve man's safety and health, and in the best interests of national defense."

How about another customer, National Cancer Institute, Washington, D. C.?

Replied James F. Kieley, information officer:

"Dr. Martin Cline, Metabolism Service . . . has been working with alligator blood in vivo in metabolisms of red blood cell production and patterns of red blood cell survival at varying metabolic rates.

"The reason for the interest in the alligator is that, like most lower vertebrates, it changes its metabolic rate with changes in temperature and environmental temperature can be changed at will.

"Alligators have also been used by the National Heart Institute in the field of cardio-vascular diseases."

Other alligators are being studied in the laboratories of the Communicable Disease Center, Public Health Service, Atlanta, Ga.

"The study," reports H. W. Richter, assistant information officer at the center, "is being done on the alligators and other reptiles in an effort

WHICH JAW HAS THE HINGE?

Few myths about the alligator and the crocodile are more common than the one which declares their jaws are hinged differently—one top, one bottom. Actually both function just like your jaws.

to determine whether these creatures harbor viruses . . . during the winter months. The studies are in fairly early stages."

This is just part of the alligator's service to mankind. McClung, for example, furnishes specimens to a number of universities and colleges, and other alligator farms do the same.

Dale Vaughn of St. Petersburg, old-time animal handler and presently executive director of the city's SPCA, has three experiences that make him somewhat special:

1) Vaughn is one of the few men that the United States War Department developed a special classification for. 2) He's also one of the few people we've found actually knocked down by an alligator's tail. 3) He can testify from personal experience to the damage a big 'gator can do in a hurry.

Originally from Elwood, Indiana, Vaughn later lived on a farm while in high school and became interested in zoology and wild life. He got a closer look in 1933-34 while serving as annoucer on a midway exhibit at the Chicago World's Fair.

"I was near Frank Buck's Jungle Show; I was fascinated by it. That's where I got acquainted with taking care of animals."

He saved his money and after the fair, went into partnership with the late F. W. Thomson, opening an animal exhibit at Chicago's Riverview Park. After a few years, the two men decided to come to Florida, which offered "the best climate in which to keep tropical animals and acclimate them for zoological exhibition in this country."

Myths and Facts

In 1937, they opened the Florida Wild Animal and Reptile Ranch in St. Petersburg, with Thomson as owner, Vaughn as manager.

"It was the city's first zoo. Although over in the Big Bayou section, an old man named Baker had about 50 'gators — many business houses in St. Petersburg had alligator eggs on display. When he went out of business, we bought his stock."

Announcing alligator wrestling, Vaughn got almost too well acquainted with the saurians. He recalls one hair-raising occasion when with an assistant he answered one of the many calls the ranch used to get, reporting a wild 'gator sporting around town:

"This one was in a little stream by Fourth Street North. He was about five or six feet long. I managed to get the lasso over his head by wading into the stream. I started to pull him toward me with the rope; he glided just like a boat.

"But I had on a pair of loose Western boots, wide at the top. I began to sink in the mud, because of the pulling. I found I was helpless, my feet were anchored and I couldn't move and the alligator was coming right toward me.

"My assistant grabbed me from behind and pulled but couldn't budge me — and we had nothing to beat the beast off with. I'd say about 60 people were lined up alongside the roadway, watching us. Fortunately, when the alligator got within about four feet of me he just lay down and didn't move. I finally just pulled my feet out of the boots and got up on dry land, then we hauled the alligator out and tied him up. That was my last time to wear short boots in a mucky area like that." (See picture on Page 56.)

Had Vaughn had his rope around a crocodile instead of an alligator, it is likely that his animal-handling career would have ended then and there.

In 1940, he was present at an accident at the Wild Animal Ranch which proved once again that a "tame" 'gator is no such thing.

"We were moving hundreds of 'gators from the old wooden pens to new cement enclosures. On this particular day, it was about quitting time and we had just hauled out of the pen the last one we intended to move — Big Bill, our largest specimen, about eight feet, 600 pounds.

"One of the men had worked with Big Bill for years, cleaning out his pen, talking to him. I heard this man say, 'I'll show you how to tie a 'gator.'"

As a rule, the loop is slipped over the brute's jaws at the end of a pole, or at least with plenty of slack between the rope-handler and the jaws. In this case the handler evidently tried to slip the rope over the snout much as you'd halter a horse.

In a flash, the huge jaws had opened and clamped down on the man's arm; the alligator went into his customary roll and tore off the arm. The victim lost much blood but survived.

"We called him Big Bad Bill after that," recalls Vaughn. "I've been knocked down by 'gators but never grabbed. You'll find that the animal uses his tail first of all to disable anything that's at that end of him, then turns around quickly and snatches it with his jaws. They've got a lot of power in that tail — I've been knocked down by a gator as small as five feet. They're much quicker than you'd think, seeing them lying there dormant."

In 1942 Vaughn was inducted into World War II and the Air Corps, in that order. Thinking to put his experience to use, he decided that fliers who might be downed in tropical jungles needed to be trained to recognize and know poisonous and dangerous reptiles and animals. A personnel officer agreed and suggested he write the War Department about it.

"This," grins Vaughn, looking back, "was about as silly a thing as an enlisted man can do. But lo and behold, the War Department approved and provided a new classification for me. A major who had served in India and knew the dangers of the jungle for the inexperienced immediately requisitioned me and I joined his staff of instructors at Lemoore Army Air Field, Fresno, California.

"I bought three alligators from an animal dealer in Texas and they were shipped to the post; I requisitioned a crocodile from the field's purchasing department but never did get it. Snakes I hunted and caught in wild areas of California. Then I had cages and pits built to contain the animals, lectured on snake bite treatment. We'd demonstrate, for example, how a soldier if startled by a snake in the jungle might expose himself to a sniper, and how they actually had nothing to fear from snakes unless they provoked an attack.

"I specialized in jungle survival. We'd make field trips to wild areas of the California mountains, catching wild duck, lizards, snakes, birds, eating what we caught. Then for a time I toured with war bond drives, using animals to attract crowds."

In 1946 Vaughn returned to St. Petersburg and went into the advertising business, which he left in 1961 to take up SPCA work. Out at the SPCA shelter there's very little alligator wrestling or rattlesnake milking to be done — but Vaughn is happy with less exotic specimens such as dogs and cats and an occasional wandering raccoon or possum!

Wildlife Officer Jim Philbin once chanced across a sight few men ever witness — a big female alligator sunning herself with half-a-dozen young crawling over her back. The female 'gator is rated one of the best reptilian mothers; a mother crocodile simply buries her eggs in a sand bank and takes off, period.

Love in 'Gator Land

RIFTING DOWN the clear, cool waters of the Weekiwachee River on Florida's Suncoast one mid-July with naturalist John Hamlet, a jovial, energetic zoologist then employed by the Weekiwachee Springs attraction on U.S. 19, we came across an unusual sight indeed.

There was an alligator pen on the river bank, its fence extending into the water to give a dozen alligators soaking room. But what really impressed us was the sight of 14 white 'gator eggs scattered about the sand at the upper side of the pen.

"I thought 'gators didn't lay eggs in captivity? Besides there's no material to make a nest out of?"

Hamlet grinned.

"The nest making is psychological, the egg-dropping is purely physical," he said. "This is July — egg-laying time."

Hamlet reached across the fence with a paddle to persuade some of the animals to climb up the bank and pose for a photo with their eggs.

There was a chorus of hissing, mighty splashing from swift flirts of the 'gator's great oar, his tail. At last, grudging cooperation. We had our picture. Soaked to the skin, we headed the boat back up-river.

Our next question was purely hopeful: "John, we've read a lot of books, talked to a lot of people. Nobody seems to know much about alligator love-making. Do you?" He did.

First, a word of explanation — alligator courtship and mating goes on mostly at evening and night time, the creature being a nocturnal type. Moreover, because this romance is carried on in considerable seclusion and swamp, it is not readily observed.

For this reason, most authorities simply assure the seeker for truth that the alligator mates in March and April, lays eggs in May and July which hatch some 60 days later, in the fall.

Hamlet had the background to make his observation — 14 years with the Biological Survey,

Love in 'Gator Land

U.S. Department of the Interior, for instance — and he had the opportunity.

Exposed to plain view on their sand-and-water cage by the Weekiwachee, the Spring's 'gators were ideal subjects, easily observed from the river.

Hamlet had made the most of his opportunity —and we feel it safe to say that he gives you the most detailed description ever heard of this little-known wilderness drama.

"All species of animals have different types of courtship," Hamlet began. "Alligators start out with bellowing in the Spring; the alligators in our pen begin the second week of May."

Romance is not instantaneous. Since seven out of ten alligators are males, this means that the lady 'gator can be choosy—and she is. She doesn't just say no, either. In some cases she will kill her suitor and begin bellowing again, sounding just as love-sick as before! And if she doesn't happen to fancy the next male, she's been known to kill him, too.

No wonder the male gets a lump in his throat when it's time to go a-courting!

Actually, says Hamlet, two pairs of muck glands, common to both sexes of all crocodilians, go into action. One pair is on the right and left sides of the lower jaw, another in the lips of the cloaca.

The glands secrete an oily substance which gives off a powerful odor offensive to humans but evidently perfume to a female gator; it serves to show her where her master lies.

"The male comes up alongside the female in water or on land," Hamlet explained. "He nudges her with his nose in her pelvic region. If she's not ready to accept him, she flirts her tail and takes off.

"When she's ready to accept him, she sidles around at right angles to his nose. He spends some time with his chin resting on any part of her body from her tail to her head, rubbing her gently with his chin.

"Then he works up to her neck and nips her in the side of the neck — a love bite. We haven't invented a thing in courtship animals haven't done before us."

Often this bite is hard enough to be painful. When the female tries to draw away, the male clamps down tighter with his jaws and works his body alongside hers.

"Then he lets go with his jaws and puts his head on top of hers, rubbing her head with his chin. He twists his body over her back to the opposite side; she twists up to meet him. The 'gator couple lies quietly for perhaps 20 minutes, then begin rolling and tumbling, their tails twisted together, legs gripping. This may continue for an hour to an hour and a half."

At last they lie quietly for ten or fifteen minutes, jaws open. Hamlet's observations of the Springs 'gators lead him to believe the mating period lasts about two months. "When man appears, they'll stop courtship immediately; in copulation they're oblivious."

Alligators do not mate with crocodiles, insofar as is known, although they are in close proximity in Florida's Everglades-Keys area. Why not?

"The courtship is different, for one thing," said Hamlet, who has observed crocodile mating in the Philippines during a "farming" attempt.

"The crocodile's courtship is purely aquatic. It consists of a great deal of chasing and nipping;

In this sand-floored pen beside the Weekiwachee River, alligators are exposed to view, have no materials with which to build nests so simply lay their eggs on the sand.

Love in 'Gator Land

the crocodile's courtship is not nearly so subtle as the alligator's, nor does it have as many stages. There's less bellowing.

"After several days, the female croc allows herself to be caught. The male gets hold of her neck as the 'gator does, but he never lets go. He comes up on the same side, but mates on that side — never goes over as the alligator does."

One question about the alligator not definitely decided is this — is he a one-gal type? You can get both yes and no answers; we're inclined to think he makes no nice distinctions.

Once mating season is over, the father departs. Some have slandered him by saying he hangs around to eat the young. This idea probably stems from the fact that the alligator feeds without regard upon anything and everything, including young if handy.

But now behold the female, considered by many as one of the finest among reptilian mammas.

Sometime during the May-July period, she will build a sizeable nest in a manner described in detail by a number of herpetologists. Selecting a

spot, she scrapes together an assortment of vegetable trash — leaves, leaf litter, stalks, stems, roots, grasses, into a large mound four to seven feet across, two to three feet high. Then she scoops out a hole in the top and lays from 29 to 68 eggs (estimates vary) with a hard, brittle shell, somewhat longer than a hen's egg.

Then the eggs are covered with more vegetable material and packed down, sometimes covered with mud on top. During the incubation period of 10 weeks, the mother is reported to wet down the nest to obtain the hot, humid conditions ideal for hatching. Some observers say she does this by carrying water in her mouth — the alligator's lower jaw is dipper-shaped.

E. A. McIlhenny, perhaps the foremost student of the creature, made temperature tests which indicated that the alligator nest was a most effective incubator.

The plant material decays and generates heat as incubation proceeds; the female guards the nest, for alligator eggs are esteemed by wild hogs, bears, raccoons and other nest-raiders. If heavy rain disturbs the nest, she'll repair it. (The fe-

What's unusual about this photo? Look closely, very closely, and you'll see mamma alligator, almost perfectly camouflaged by nature, guarding her nest. See? (Nest is mound of earth and pine needles at left center; alligator just right of center at top of photo.) Fortunately, you hear the mother's warning hiss in plenty of time to detour. Another few steps and she would probably have charged Times photographer Jack Ramsdell. Picture was made at Godwin's Gatorland near Kissimmee.

Love in 'Gator Land

male, may use the same nest year after year, merely adding a little more material.)

Next occurs one of the most interesting phases of all. One bright day from within the nest there comes curious sound — a high-pitched grunting which brings the mother on the run. This is the signal of the young ones, their six to eight inches neatly coiled inside the eggs, that they are ready to see the world.

The mother will scrape away the top of the nest, if it is too closely packed for them to penetrate. The little one is equipped with an "egg tooth," temporarily attached to the end of his snout, with which to break out of his shell.

Once out in the world, they head instinctively for water — and they're already capable of biting with a set of needle-like teeth.

The baby alligator will be lucky if he survives, for many enemies regard him as a tasty morsel: Black bass, heron, bullfrogs, cottonmouth moccasins, otters, raccoons, mink, larger alligators and other creatures.

One reason that the young survive is mamma alligator. Following the hatching, she keeps them in a shallow pool while she stands guard or stays in the vicinity to give them protection, for a period of about 18 months until the young animals have become big enough to fend for themselves.

Hunters can attest the truth of this. A method used in the old days was to catch a small alligator and squeeze him to make him give his distress call — a high-pitched grunt. Usually this is enough to bring the mother charging to attack.

After hatching, usually in late summer or early fall, the baby alligator has enough of the egg yolk left in his body to keep him alive for six or eight months, Drysdale and Usina of the St. Augustine Alligator Farm say. Thus he may winter without food in the mother's den, though she makes no attempt to feed him.

By the time he attains sexual maturity at the age of six years, Mr. 'Gator is ready to find romance in a mild March night himself — and start the life cycle up again.

Owen Godwin, owner of Godwin's Gatorland, exhibits gator egg taken from nest. A number of his females make nests near the farm's lake each summer; Godwin has raised a good many small alligators from these nests.

Clad only in his derby hat and his vest, Joe rode the alligator across the pond like a cowboy standing up — only to meet up with an overhanging limb!

The Old-Timers

HEN DID THE FIRST MAN muster up enough raw courage to dive into a pool of water and grapple with an alligator in tne latter's native element?

No one will ever know for sure, of course. But the late Albert DeVane, old-time naturalist of Lake Placid, Florida, had a pretty good idea. His research indicated that it may have been one Alligator Plott, member of a family which pioneered in the limestone and pineland areas now known as DeSoto, Hardie and Manatee Counties.

Plott, a notable alligator hunter back in the 1870s and 1880s, evidently preferred the submarine approach:

"He would dive into a hole on Horse Creek, come up under his alligator, tackle him and bring him out. He probably learned this act from the Seminoles."

DeVane knows more about the Florida Indian's relations with the alligator than any white man living, for he is a long-time friend of Seminole leader Billy Bowlegs. (A name about as common among the Seminoles as Smith is among whites, for some obscure reason.)

Bowlegs, an old man of uncertain years, seems to bear out the theory that the alligator was to the Florida Indian of the 1700-1800 period and before, what the buffalo was to the Plains Indian of the West.

Just as the Sioux took time out to paint pictures of the buffalo, so the Florida Indians carved and painted likenesses of the alligator. The now extinct Calusa Indians of the Key Marco area in Southwestern Florida left behind fifteenth-century wood carving unequalled in Indian art.

A fine specimen on view at the University of Pennsylvania Museum, Philadelphia, is a wooden alligator head, 10¼ inches long. Authorities say the work is marked by a sensitive realism not found elsewhere in wood sculpture north of Mexico. Wet muck preserved this carving over the centuries. Fortunately, it was made of a wood which withstood the strain of drying, after it was excavated in 1895 by F. H. Cushing.

Like the buffalo, the alligator spelled food to the savage.

Sitting in long and friendly pow-wow, DeVane and Bowlegs explored the latter's memory of the old days, and the stories the Seminole had heard of grandfathers when he was a child.

"Alligator eggs," DeVane reported, "were a great source of food, Billy Bowlegs said, especially just following the last (Seminole) war.

"They gathered the eggs from the nests and boiled or roasted them in ashes.

"The eggs were tested in water, Billy said: 'If egg go deep to bottom me keep 'em, eat 'em. If egg float or partly float me put egg back in nests.'"

The Old-Timers

Eating habits differed with various tribal units, however, the old Seminole said.

Some of the Big Cypress Indians ate alligator tail; Billy's people, the Tallahassee Creeks, never did. Billy's people ate panther; the Big Cypress Indians never did.

"From 1880 until 1910," DeVane said, "the alligator hide was the Seminoles medium of exchange, his greatest source of revenue." (This was the period in which thousands of alligators were being slaughtered by Florida's frontiersmen.)

Most primitive people use animals as medicine in some way or another, and the Seminoles were no exception.

"Long time ago," Billy Bowlegs told his white friend, "me medicine man. Get alligator about 18 to 24 inches long, kill him, put close to fire get hot, but not cooked."

Then the 'gator's warm belly was placed on the stomach of an Indian suffering with "belly ache."

Here we have the alligator in an entirely new role — as hot water bottle!

By invitation, (a rare honor) DeVane has witnessed several of the Seminole dances. One of the main figures is the Alligator Dance.

"The figures or execution of this dance is very much different from any other dance; a song is sung during the dance, the meaning of it I do not know," DeVane said. (As a rule such dances act out the hunting and killing of the animal in question.)

Legends, myths about the alligator? Billy Bowlegs only shook his head. These there may have been — who can say? But it is doubtful that a Seminole will tell a white man, no matter how old a friend, all that is in his mind. And scholars know that the record of customs and traditions of the old ones here in Florida are far from complete.

"Apparently the legendry, superstitions, and ceremonial significance of the alligator in connection with the Seminoles has largely disappeared," says Frank W. Long, business management advisor to the Seminole Tribe of Dania Reservation at Okalee Indian Village on Florida's East Coast.

Talking with Billy Osceola, chairman of the tribal Council, Long learned that Seminoles consider the alligator a relative of the poisonous snakes: "Probably," comments Long, "because its bite usually became infected . . . and the victim died as a result."

The alligator, said Osceola, was not sacred among the old ones but greatly respected and never killed wantonly. However, there was no compunction against hide-hunting when a market developed in the 1800s.

Osceola recalls that the alligator was used as a clan totem or symbol, as were other animals. The alligator was feared, but not abnormally. Caution was used where the creature was concerned, and children were always forbidden to go near areas where alligators were thick; babies were especially protected.

One thing is evident. The alligator, down through the years, has been a definite asset to the Seminole in the latter's constant battle for survival. Every time you see an Indian brave wrestle an alligator at a roadside attraction, you're seeing that same old business association, still in action!

One of the most interesting collections of true 'gator stories from Florida's early times, when the reptiles were common as cows, can be found in "Pioneer Florida," edited by the late D. B. McKay, distinguished editor of The Tampa Tribune and a mighty hunter in his own right. The book is a compilation of newspaper columns appearing in the Tribune over a period of over 12 years on the "Pioneer Florida" page, a most popular feature, written and edited by McKay in his 80s and 90s.

One remarkable story is about "the best storyteller in Florida," one Joe Culbreath, as related by oldtime printer Charles N. Bardin, Sr.

Camped on the shores of a large pond near Tampa many years ago, Joe decided to do a little night fishing, although the rest of his party was busy fighting mosquitoes.

"He stripped off his clothing except a vest and his derby. The vest was necessary to carry his cigars, matches and bacon rind baits. The band of the derby carried his extra hooks. He walked out into that dark pond until the water came up to where 'the Indian shot him' — just below the vest."

On the bottom, Joe felt what he thought was a log with rough bark. He stood on it and began casting. A big fish was hooked and as he was pulling it in the "log" began moving—he stood atop a big alligator which had seen the struggling fish and decided to dine.

Things happened fast. The alligator took after the fish, with Joe atop the 'gator's back. The fish made for the opposite shore and jumped from the water to dry land. Joe was knocked off the alligator's back by the limb of an overhanging tree. But he waded ashore and secured the fish, which he exhibited to the party as evidence of his adventure. (Skeptics may doubt that a man could balance atop an alligator rushing through the water, but when it comes to swapping good stories, we have no use for doubters.)

McKay's family refugeed at Seffner, Fla., during the yellow fever epidemic in 1876; he was

The Old-Timers

eight at the time. Over the gulf of years, he still recalled bringing in the cows. Now many a farm boy has brought in the cows at evening—but not under such circumstances.

It was a daily adventure, McKay wrote, because the trip passed through a big prairie almost entirely under water, ranging from a few inches to several feet, studded with alligator holes:

"Alligators of all sizes, from monsters 10 and 12 feet long to the recently hatched babies — were in sight always. 'Buddy' (Columbus) the youngest of the Stafford sons (a family with which the McKays were staying) apparently had little fear of even the largest of the reptiles. He carried a big oak club, and I saw him many times slip up on a big one sleeping in the sun and crack it on the head with that club — of course always keeping out of range of that deadly tail."

Florida's old-timers had a lot of respect for the alligator, however — tough people themselves, they admired toughness, and no creature was so tough as the alligator. Once, one nearly derailed a train and then did battle with the engineer!!

McKay's authority on this is outdoorsman 'Frog' Smith.

The time was a half-century ago, when a 15-foot 'gator was nothing to get excited about, they were so common in Florida. The little B.C.& St. A. passenger train ran from Chipley to Southport, Fla., Smith recalls, and on this occasion was pulled by No. 22, an old-time engine with four high drivers. "Big Six" Williams was the engineer.

Coming through Sweetwater Swamp, Williams spotted a nine-foot alligator sunning himself on the narrow roadbed, right across the track. He threw on the brakes but it was too late:

"Old 22 danced and trembled as she hit the alligator and rolled over him, while the tender went into the air and rocked wildly as it stopped with the 'gator wedged under the rear truck. Though mussed up some from being rolled under the engine and with part of his tail gone, the 'gator was still full of fight and gave the city passengers quite a show before 'Big Six' finally got a lucky swing with a sledge hammer." (In those days engineers carried their own repair tools just in case.)

The old-time alligator hunter was a determined soul. Once he was in action, it took a mighty sly or husky creature to escape with a whole skin. Consider 'Frog' Smith's story of Joe Payne and Bill Finch, two hunters who were out night hunting in West Florida when they spotted a big target, dazzled him with a spotlight and shot him.

It was customary to make sure of a 'dead' 'gator by chopping it behind the head with an axe. Finch, who was doing the paddling, ran their 14-foot skiff up beside the floating alligator. Payne stood up with the axe and swung lustily. But the deceptive shadows caused him to overshoot and in he went over the 'gator, axe, light and all!

The animal suddenly came to life and slapped the boat over with his powerful tail; Finch went over on the other side. Both men floundered in waist-deep water in the dark, with the threshing alligator for a companion.

Finch swung the axe but the deceptive shadows caused him to overshoot and he tumbled into the water over the alligator, axe, **headlamp and all!**

The Old-Timers

Payne was able to quickly relight his carbide lamp. Its eerie glow revealed Finch and the alligator, both making for shore. Finch had grabbed up the boat gig and pursued the wounded brute, finally spearing it in the side. Payne splashed ashore with the gun but the powder was wet and wouldn't fire. He hurried back and felt for the axe, finally dispatching their quarry. When they loaded the reptile for the trip home, Smith declares, they found he was just three feet longer than their 14-foot boat!

McKay rates this as the 'grandpappy of all alligator stories,' told by one T. J. LaVeigne of Clermont, Fla.

Near Clermont, he said, there once lived a man, his wife and daughter. They lived by raising and selling grapes and wine. When the vineyard was young they had found a small alligator on the grounds and raised it for a pet.

Over the years the animal became very tame, was given the run of the front yard and spent most of his time sleeping in the shade of a large guava bush.

"But should a customer or visitor come to the place," LaVeigne said, "he was instantly awake and would give the alarm by his hoarse grunts. Then he would make for the vineyard where the family were at work and would not cease his grunts until he saw one of them start to the house. Then he would return to the bed under the guava bush and resume his interrupted nap. Many people went to the place to verify the stories they had heard of an alligator that filled the place of a yard dog."

The mother of the family had charge of him, and he was said to be so fond of her that he grew restless if she was absent from the place for a few hours. He learned to open screen doors and even the solid inner doors, seeking his mistress. On one occasion, when she became ill, he was found asleep beside her bed.

Net fishermen dislike to take certain large specimens such as shark — they tear up the net trying to escape. And it is even worse when you catch alligators! The McKay book cites F. W. Myers of Mulberry on this point. Myers told of an occasion long ago on Watermelon Lake, really an arm of Lake Okeechobee. The men laid out their seine in water three feet deep and began a circle.

"I saw an alligator climb over the corks, then another — I counted four. Well, I thought, that's a relief . . ."

As the net was nearly closed, the fish entrapped therein began acting up. Another alligator, about nine feet long, was keeping them company. Bill Hendry, one of the fishermen, grabbed the reptile by the snout so it couldn't open its jaw. The alligator began to roll and was tangled up in the seine in short order; so was Bill. But Myers caught one of the 'gator's front legs and stopped the rolling, then the fishermen killed it with a pocket knife by stabbing the back of the head to sever the spinal cord.

One may wonder why men would risk their lives against a creature so well-equipped with teeth, so powerful. Money, as always, had a good deal to do with it. An item from the Bartow Courier-Informant of Oct. 25, 1905, cited by McKay tells us that one Bill Brown's big ox wagon came in from Big Cypress store on Tuesday with 1,270 'gator hides: "Bill sold his hides to R. A. Henderson, receiving a little over $1,000 for this three weeks haul of hides." And in 1905, remember, the dollar was a very healthy piece of money.

Lake dwellers in Florida these days are not unaccustomed to hearing a 'gator or two bellowing during mating season. But the old, old timers say that this is a pale echo of the mighty choruses that used to go booming forth. The late Judge E. C. May of Inverness, long-time Floridian, wrote McKay this comment:

"I was raised in alligator country and primitive surroundings, and I heard and saw much of alligators since my earliest recollection. The flat cypress ponds, creeks and rivers that surrounded our farm were full of them, and their hideous bellowing would often fill the morning air."

He recalled one spring morning in particular when he was about eight years old that a bull alligator in Ten Mile Creek began roaring and was answered by another from a pond on the other side of the field in which he was hoeing corn.

"At once both were in full chorus and the air over our cornfield was filled with the frightful sound . . ."

But the boy was not afraid — "at least, not much." He had been taught that alligators were not dangerous if one stayed out of the water.

Outdoorsman 'Frog' Smith is quoted by McKay as rating alligator steak highly. As a young man, Smith operated the commissary of a railroad being built to a phosphate town near Fort Meade by several hundred Negro and Italian laborers. Alligators made a frequent target along the track. Whenever Smith would bag one not over seven feet long, one of the shovel gang would cut off the tail just behind the legs and the steak would be served that night. "It looked and tasted," Smith said, "much like steaks cut from a big kingfish."

The pioneers are gone now. But the alligator is still around, and he hasn't changed a bit since granddad's day. A hundred or a thousand years from now, the swamp dragon will still be around, an object of curiosity to our great-great-great grandchildren.

Hunting alligators sounds like going out to shoot a lion. But the fact that so many 'gator hunters have lived to tell the tale proves that the saurian is basically peaceable.

The Hunters

NCE AND FOR ALL," we said, "just how fast can a 'gator go on land? Some of the books say he can outrun a man for a hundred yards; others, that they can make a considerable show of speed for a short distance. Other naturalists claim the alligator is uncoordinated and clumsy when he tries to run—or that he's easily avoided on land."

Two 'gator hunters exchanged broad grins.

"I've seen hundreds of them," said the late Jim Philbin, 18 years a Wildlife Officer with the Florida Game and Fresh Water Fish Commission. "And they can move—run as fast as a man. I've seen them run 40, 50 feet to get out of the way. They may look like they're clumsy but they're not."

Few people have ever seen an alligator in a hurry, which may explain the mistaken notion that he's slow. But the fact is, Mr. 'Gator doesn't crawl when he's anxious to move — he hoists his cigar-shaped body up on those stubby legs and GOES.

Bob Pixton, St. Petersburg body shop operator whose life-long hobby has been alligators, agreed. A grown alligator can travel as fast as a running man for a distance — but the creature is usually running the other way.

Jim and Bob know what they're talking about. Both have dealt with the Florida alligator for years — Jim professionally, Bob as a hobby.

Jim Philbin, physically, was a small, lean man, tough as a palmetto root, who remembered the old days of hunting, when $1 a hide was the going rate. His hunting companion, Bob Pixton, is a dark haired, younger version of Jim. Both have built-in tans from years in the outdoors, and both have the kind of king-size nerve it takes to hunt alligators.

They serve a special purpose in fast growing Pinellas county, where people keep piling in and alligators won't acknowledge it, claiming squatter's rights.

"Phone's liable to ring anytime, even at night," said Jim. "Somebody's got an alligator around

The Hunters

their house or yard and wants you to come get him right away — they're scared. We get at least a dozen calls a month here in Pinellas County."

Just how do you capture an alligator?

Bob, who grew up in Tampa and began tagging along on alligator hunts as a youngster, with his dad, says it's simple. (He assists the Commission men in this chore when they're busy elsewhere, has a special permit that allows him to take any alligator specified, by any means.)

Bob's chief weapon is a length of pipe with an airplane cable running through it, a noose on the business end.

"All you do," he said, "is slip the noose around the 'gator's neck and tighten it. Then you can hold him away while he raises a fuss. Some of them quiet right down, some don't. It's just like fighting a big old bass."

Then, while somebody else holds the pole and noosed alligator, you go up in front of him and close his jaws, tie them with rope or masking tape.

"You could almost tie them with a thread," put in Jim. "You can hold them shut with two fingers. Alligator's got muscle to close 'em but not to open."

So your captive's mouth is shut and he's quieted down. What then?

"Some people tie their legs, front and back, or throw a sack over their eyes to help quiet them down," Bob said. "I don't. Just put them in the trunk of my car."

Ross Allen, at right, demonstrates for the benefit of his three husky sons — John, Tom and Robert, from left to right — that a frontal approach with both hands holding the jaws closed is best with a alligator of this size. Fact that alligator's jaw opening muscles are comparatively weak has kept a lot of handlers intact over the years.

The Hunters

The back seat is not so good. One game warden tried it and left the car for a minute. When he came back, the 'gator had stuck his bony snout through the glass of the window! The captured gator is usually taken to the nearest roadside zoo.

"An alligator," explained Bob, "is not going to hurt anybody unless you get them cornered. If she's a mother with little ones, yes — but as a rule they're just as scared of you as you are of them."

The hunters agree that for commercial purposes, the alligator has been given a terrible reputation he doesn't deserve.

With people flocking to Florida's lakes and rivers where the alligator abounds, the saurian has ample opportunity to attack if he wants to: "There'd be people killed once a week if they were mean and vicious," said Bob. But neither he nor Jim, in many years of experience, have ever heard of a fatal attack. "I've been nailed twice, but both of them had reason," said Bob.

"Once when I was about 13 a bunch of us cornered one about four feet long in a culvert. We held a net over one end and I crawled in the other. He started by me. I caught him by the mouth, and then reached for his leg — that was my mistake. He reached around and caught me by the arm. I backed out of the culvert, he dropped off and got away. I carried the marks for years.

"Another time, I was called out to pick up an alligator under a house trailer. They'd been punching him with a pole and he was mad. I got down beside the trailer and he came out and tore the top off my shoe — I'd just bought them a few days before, too. My wife was mad about that."

If you ever plan to grab an alligator by the tail, don't. Despite his looks, he has lightning-like reflexes: "He'll turn around and eat you up," said Bob, sincerely. (A recent travel film on South America illustrated this point. It showed a group of caimans — called the South American alligator — basking on a river bank. A man stepped forward and shouted. Quicker than thought, the seemingly sluggish reptiles swapped ends and vanished into the water.)

Bob once had a hair-raising experience few hunters would enjoy. He and Jim were prowling through alligator country one dark night when he stepped on top of a 'gator den and the dirt roof caved in, dumping Bob down into the cave itself.

"I went in head over heels," grinned Bob. "Never did find out if a 'gator was there but you should have seen me come out."

The alligator den, by the bank of a pond or stream, is a prime target for hunters. Usually

What's it like, holding a pole with a noose at the end firmly around the neck of an angry seven-foot alligator? "Just like fighting a big old bass," says Bob Pixton, who catches bothersome alligators around St. Petersburg.

there are marks of a "crawl" around, a track worn through the grass and weeds; perhaps a spot where the 'gator suns himself. There may be a mound to indicate the top of the den, which is dug a little below the water line and may be 10 to 15 feet deep, of similar width. (An old 'gator's den, which he may enlarge each year, may be as long as 40 feet.)

"You use an 18 to 20 foot pole with a hook on the end," explained Jim. "You feel around; 98 percent of the time if he's there you'll feel him. When you do, you snatch it." The hooked, struggling 'gator is then dragged up through the entrance and knocked on the head, a process requiring equal amounts of strength and nerve since the animal doesn't like it.

The den, whose entrance may or may not be under the water, serves as headquarters for the alligator's territory but the hunters don't think he hibernates there: "We see them all winter long." Perhaps Florida winters are too much like summer? This point is not clear but it is known that

The Hunters

in captivity on Florida alligator farms, the creature does not hibernate.

Jim Philbin remembers way back to stories of the old-time hunters, when a man might kill a couple of dozen alligators a night, fire-hunting: "They used a lard-oil bullseye lantern," he said. "Stink? Smoke? It'd give you a headache! But it kept the skeeters away. It gave a dim light — the eyes would show up a pretty ruby red."

"How come a lot of people say they're orange?"

"Brighter the light, the brighter the eye," explained Jim. "It's illegal now to use a headlight and gun for any purpose."

Night hunting (prior to the ban on alligator hunting Sept. 2, 1961) was still done with a powerful light strapped to the hunter's head — but he was equipped with either a noose-pole or a harpoon — not a gun.

Moving silently through the waters, the hunter stands in the prow waiting for those two orange coals to show up in his beam; the paddler moves the boat as quietly as possible. The hunter using a noose — usually heavy wire run through a light, strong pipe — seeks to ease it over the head of the momentarily dazzled alligator on the surface a few feet from the boat.

In another method the harpoon man has a trident fixed to a pole. A strong rope is attached to the trident head. When he comes within range, the hunter seeks to lodge the trident prongs in the alligator's shoulder. The trident sticks, if he aims well, and becomes detached from the spear pole. Then as the alligator whirls he obligingly bundles himself up in the line, allowing capture.

In both cases the alligator is brought alongside the boat and pulled into it if he's not too big — otherwise he's towed to the nearest bank to be trussed up.

Watching an alligator being noosed, you might wonder why the loop isn't tightened around his snout instead of around his neck. There's a very simple reason. Because the snout tapers, the swamp dragon would have no trouble in pushing the restraining noose off with his front feet. But once anchored behind the big jaws, the rope is firmly seated. Then the hunter, with no little skill, may throw a neat half-hitch over the jaws and proceed from there.

The alligator's muscular, heavy tail is dangerous and can knock you kicking. But the dangerous end by far is the one equipped with those huge and powerful jaws.

Once alligator hunters used a horse to help with the skinning, after 'gators were stacked like cordwood following a good night's hunting.

One dark night alligator hunter Bob Pixton was moving through the swampland when he stepped on the roof of an alligator den and plunged down into the cave itself!

"They'd hook the rope on the saddle horn, other end fixed to the hide under the chin," Jim said. "Horse would keep a tension on the skin, make it easier to take off."

How long does it take to skin an alligator? Thirty minutes for an experienced hand — four hours for an amateur. Often the skinner will encounter bullets, proof of the 'gator's hardihood.

Only about two-thirds of the alligator hide is used. The skinner cuts down along the sides, using these and the pliable belly skin; the armored back, with its bony "scutes" is of no value for leather.

About the biggest alligator Jim Philbin ever tackled was a huge 14-footer in a St. Petersburg creek. He got the noose around the giant's neck all right but couldn't haul the creature's 450 pounds of muscle out.

The Hunters

"I was by myself," he said, "so I got a kid to run up to my car and bring my gun. I shot the alligator under the cap."

The "cap," he explained, is the ridge just behind the eyes that sits on the top of the skull, the spot where the saurian is most vulnerable. "Old timers," he said, "used to shoot them through the side with a .22 — most pro hunters use a .22. It'd make the gator sick, and he'd come out on the bank. Then they'd knock him in the head."

Does the alligator feel pain? Tom Helm, outdoor writer and naturalist of Clearwater, Florida, in his book, "Shark," says that after a thorough study he is convinced that cold-blooded creatures have no sense of pain.

"Frequently I have seen sharks hooked time and again and still coming back for more punishment," Helm notes. He writes of cases in which fatally-wounded sharks have continued to feed as though nothing had happened. On another occasion a 12-foot white shark, shot through the top of the head with a .30-.30 Winchester rifle, showed no signs of life when hauled on board a shrimp trawler.

He was tossed back into the water — and 15 minutes later, caught again!

The brain is the only vital organ of the shark that can result in instant death if damaged, Helm concludes. But, situated in the middle of the head and well protected on all sides, it presents a difficult target.

The alligator presents an interesting parallel. Alligator farm operators have seen them lose a leg or part of the tail in a fight and a few minutes later be contentedly sunning themselves again. (Wild alligators are often taken, missing leg or tail, or bearing other marks of combat.)

Like the shark, the alligator seems instantly vulnerable only in his small brain, centered on his broad, flat head behind the eyes — and veteran hunters aim at the base of this "cap."

Another method of alligator hunting is "fishing." A large hook baited with aged fish is used, attached to a powerful line. Often the alligator will gulp it. Should he escape, for any reason, it doesn't seem to bother him; Jim and Bob swear his digestive juices will dissolve metal!

Of all alligators big and little, the hunters agree, a six-footer is the toughest to handle. He's not big enough to be sluggish, but he's big enough to be dangerous — and amazingly fast on his feet.

One of the meanest they've ever met up with was a blind one, both eyes shot out but still getting along somehow. Another Bob captured prov-

His boots stuck in the mud, Vaughn found the alligator moving toward him in the water.

ed to be a real surprise — when the alligator opened his jaws he didn't have a tooth in his head!

A nocturnal creature, the alligator spends most of the day basking in the sun. His mouth may be open. One reason for this is the leeches that attach themselves to the softer portions of the skin, even inside the mouth. The sun dries the pests up — but the water revives them again.

Summertime is alligator time in Florida. The reptiles were protected during their mating and egg-laying season, February through May, but beginning June 1st the eight-month open season allowed any alligator six feet or over to be taken, prior to the ban on all hunting. Alligator hunting was the state's unknown industry; don't forget that an estimated 18,835 specimens were taken during the year 1959-60 for a direct profit of $343,887.50, according to the State Game and Fresh Water Fish Commission. Average price, $2.50 a foot. In Pinellas County alone, 60 permits were issued in the summer of 1961 — and Pinellas is just one of Florida's 67 counties.

A lot of people, Jim Philbin said, just wanted to get one 'gater to mount. But a lot of other outdoorsmen got the habit. It was a thrilling sport—with financial reward thrown in.

The Unsafe Saurians

E'VE DONE HUNDREDS of interviews in our newspapering career—but one of the strangest wasn't with a lady wrestler, an archeologist digging up Indian skeletons nor yet a slightly wacky inventor. Just two nice retired folks, living in a nice little home out on the south side of St. Petersburg back in the summer of 1952.

You could tell something was different as soon as you walked into the living room. That difference amounted to two active, healthy four-foot five-inch long alligators running around the house.

As soon as we learned that they had no appetite for writer's shank, we "met" Butch and Peter as they perched on their owner's knees. But evidently we weren't projecting the right vibrations. The sizeable whitish mouths gaped wide, the yellowish eyes looked threatening and a hiss like that of a good-sized locomotive told us to keep our distance.

These two specimens, had been acquired when they were six inches long. For four years their owners had carefully kept growth charts. Fed meats and shrimp twice a week in summer, once a week in winter, Butch and Peter grew at the rate of 11½ inches a year — a bit more than a young one in the wild grows.

The owners, (who preferred to remain anonymous) had found that the reptiles grew twice as fast in summer. Only thing added to the diet was calcium, which wild alligators evidently obtain from the bones of animals and fish.

Because of the neighbors' nerves, Butch and Peter were house pets. Even so, they remained creatures of the night.

In hot summer weather, one might be soaking in the bathtub in daytime while the other snoozed under the bed. At night, they moved about quite a bit. Some might feel it a bit nerve-wrecking, the sound of a reptilian body slithering across a hardwood floor in the night, but the couple were used to it.

Certainly a neighborhood dog will never forget the house or alligators. He happened to be inspecting the premises one fine morning while Butch was in the living room. The dog strolled by the screen door, unsuspecting, and in a flash the alligator flung himself toward the door (locked, fortunately.)

The visiting canine fell backwards down the steps but managed to land in running position and departed under forced draft. (This seemed a good place to note that 'gators do not, contrary to belief, have a special appetite for dogs. They have a special appetite for anything.)

One of the most interesting points about Butch and Peter was this; their owners declared they were completely housebroken. This would seem to indicate that the alligator is not as dumb as he is made out to be by some observers.

Since Florida now forbids the sale of baby alligators, you don't find many cases like this.

But a good many people have casual friendships with good-sized alligators, with food the common bond.

The "tame" 'gator is fairly common. He's usually a lake or pond dweller. Somebody starts feeding him scraps. Like most other animals, the 'gator is smart enough to return to the same spot in hope of more hand-outs; in fact, he'll come when called.

The Unsafe Saurians

At a sausage and meat factory in Tampa, for instance, a nearby alligator learned to come for raw hamburger and grew with amazing rapidity. Golfers at Naples Beach Golf Club "raised" a two-footer to five feet at his water hole home on the 18th fairway.

Down on the Myakka River, Mr. and Mrs. Robert Rose of Camp Playmor had a "mascot" of years standing — "Al," a 13-foot whopper. He grew so accustomed to civilization that he'd spend the night on the warm concrete ramp in front of the camp building. (Early morning fishermen who didn't know of Al's habits sometimes got a rather nasty shock.)

Food, of course, was the big attraction. Al specialized in disposing of fish waste tossed into the water by anglers.

One day an 80-pound dog vanished and although Al looked as innocent as an alligator can look, State Conservation officers hauled him far up the river to Myakka State Park. In three days, Al was back at camp with a friendly grin for all. He was finally speared, then shot at, became insulted and left for good.

It would seem that alligators do remember to some extent. Jim Philbin, Florida Game and Fresh Water Fish Commission wildlife officer, captured a big alligator in a St. Petersburg creek several years ago. The 10-footer has been viewed by thousands as he suns his enormous grayish-

Life has few nastier shocks for an unsuspecting dog than the discovery that a large alligator is the pet the neighbors have running around the living room.

An 80-pound dog vanished one day and the saurian mascot of the fish camp was suspectetd.

black bulk atop a mound in his special pen at St. Petersburg's Lake Maggiore Park nature trail.

Ordinarily, the big alligator ignores all comments as he lies still as a statue while visitors peer through the wire fence, 20 feet away. But when Philbin, the man who captured him, showed up by the fence, "Henry" suddenly came to life. Hissing with fury, he plunged off his island into the water, swam across the pond and climbed up the bank to where Philbin stood. It had been two years since the wildlife officer had captured him — but the alligator hadn't forgotten. "All I did," grins Jim, "was to give him a good home."

Those who know the brute best are in hearty agreement on one point. Feeding a saurian should not get into the hand-out stage if he's more than a couple of feet long. His mouth is just not built for polite bites, which is why sensible people toss him snacks or hand them out on the end of a stick.

Long-time hunters say frankly that they fear "tame" alligators. They argue that the reptile's actions are unpredictable and that once accustomed to getting food, the beast can turn mean if denied it.

The Unsafe Saurians

Vane L. Farnsworth of St. Petersburg coaxes "Joe" his pet 'gator up on the latter's feeding stand. This nine-footer is one of the most photographed alligators in Florida. (Picture was taken a decade ago when Joe was only a little seven-footer.)

In a pond behind his home on his five-acre farm just outside St. Petersburg, Vane L. Farnsworth, one-time cookie manufacturer from Cuba, N. Y., maintains an unusual pet—a nine-foot alligator named Joe.

Drive out to the farm and amiable Van Farnsworth drops what he's doing, digs a package of chicken necks out of the refrigerator and guides you to the edge of a pretty 300-foot long pond, some 25 yards from the back door.

"Hey Joe!" he yells.

The silent greenish-brown waters at our feet stir. And all of a sudden there's Joe, dripping and homely, waddling up the bank toward his feeding platform. He's illustrating a basic point with alligator pets — there's just one bond of friendship between reptile and human and that is food.

The platform is a little stepladder of planks about three feet high. Farnsworth stands on one side, the chicken necks held high. Joe pauses at the bottom, sullenly, and then at his master's urging, scrambles up the steps. He stops half-way up

and his whitish, cavernous mouth gapes open, revealing a chilling collection of jagged teeth.

Farnsworth drops the chicken in. The jaws crunch shut; Joe swings down from the platform, and like a coon with food heads for the pond to dive in and chomp his mouthful. Then he's back for more.

"Watch this," says Farnsworth.

He picks up a cane pole and baits up with a bread ball. In a minute a fat little fish is flopping about on the grass.

"Get him, Joe."

The saurian has been waiting by his master's feet, watching the fishing with the cold, inhuman stare of a desk clerk in a ritzy hotel regarding a late arrival with no baggage. At the words, he hoists himself up and hunches over in the ungainly alligator gait to where the fish lies. A quick sideways movement of the snout and the fish is gone.

"Funny thing happened," says Farnworth reflectively. "He'll eat vegetables, likes left-over grits and rice. The other day, I brought a man

The Unsafe Saurians

Risky photo. Owen Godwin, owner of Gatorland near Kissimmee, Fla., was so proud upon acquiring this huge Florida Crocodile that he posed for this picture and nearly lost his life doing it. As he released the great jaws and leaped to one side, the crocodile swung around and narrowly missed its snap at Godwin's flying boot. At 14 feet, 3 inches, "Old Bonecrusher", who died in 1970, was believed to have been the world's largest captive crocodile. Godwin has refused offers of $5,000 from zoos for the huge specimen.

with white shoes out here. Joe started toward him — first time he ever went toward a person that way. The man hopped up on a bench, and Joe stopped. We think he figured those white shoes were grits."

"The only thing he won't eat," Mrs. Farnsworth says, "is baked goods. Spits out bread every time."

"But we still don't know if he's Joe or Josephine," Mrs. Farnsworth says. "We've never heard him bellow. Every year about the last of June he disappears for about a month. In winter he goes under the bank of the pond into his den and we don't see much of him. He's afraid of children; soon as he hears them he takes off. Same with guns. When dove hunting season comes, the sound of the guns seems to send him into hiding."

The Farnsworths are careful not to feed Joe at the back door — but always by the pond side.

"I don't want to walk out the back door some night and step on him," smiles Mrs. F.

Another much-photographed alligator in the St. Petersburg area is Albert, a 12-footer who rules Lake Veronica at Conrad Mobile Park, 9333 Park Blvd., across from Seminole Country Club. Back in 1956 the Conrad brothers, Ross and Fred, adopted him and began feeding him. So did trailer park residents. Albert grew and grew—so much so that some people worried.

Mrs. Hedwig C. Conrad, mother of Ross and Fred, got in touch with game authorities and got permission to keep Albert (along with his girl friend Alberta) if the Conrads would put a fence around the lake and get a permit.

As a result, it's just one big happy family, with Albert posing happily for tourist cameras daily. Maybe he knows he's probably the largest "tame" 'gator in all of Florida!

Veteran hunters and animal men say the "tame" 'gator never was. Some are less wild, is all.

Crocodilian As A Pet

BIG CROCODILIAN PETS create nervous owners — and are apt to break the furniture with their tails, in addition to giving the postman a bad time. So most people who go in for these unusual pets like the little ones, eight inches to a foot long.

At one time visitors to the Southeast shipped baby alligators back home — but in recent years Florida laws have put them under state protection. As a result the novelty trade imports enormous numbers of caiman, (usually the Spectacled Caiman, commonest crocodilian) from northern South America's streams and rivers.

He is correctly known as "South American Alligator."

An idea of the extent of this trade comes from G. L. Thompson of the Lane Wilson Company, Monroe, La., world-wide distributors of pet reptiles.

Thompson says his firm obtains caimans through importers in the Miami area, and ships about 500 South American alligators per week to pet shops and variety stores across the nation. Shipping season is from May 15th until early October, since the animals are not available during the winter months.

When you consider that this is just one firm, you realize a great many people must be interested in these little characters.

Zoos around the nation can testify to the popularity of crocodilian pets; they get the ones that have outgrown pethood.

Comments Herndon G. Dowling, curator of reptiles at the New York Zoological Society Park, (Bronx Zoo, N. Y.):

"We do receive a rather large number of crocodilians (mostly caimans but a few alligators) from people who have received them as pets and then are unable to care for them. About 100 per year come to us in this fashion.

"I do not believe that this indicates very closely the extent of the pet trade for this area, however, since I believe that we receive a relatively small percentage of the animals that actually come to New York."

The zoo offers one of the best assortments of crocodilians on view in the nation — some 75 individuals of 15 species.

A young alligator is more docile, less snappish than a young caiman. The young alligator has a black ground color, with faint crossbands, while adults are dark brown to blackish in color, with faint crossbands in some cases.

A young caiman is light brown or gray with distinct black, quite narrow crossbands, The Spectacled Caiman gets his name from the fact that his eyelid is more heavily ridged, and connected be-

Crocodilian as a Pet

tween the eyes like the bridge of a pair of spectacles.

The South American alligator may resent handling and be difficult to feed. However, he presents a challenge — and many owners have found that with patience their particular beastie can become a reasonably contented pet.

Suppose you've decided you're going to own one of these hangovers from the dinosaur era. You go to the pet shop — and what do you look for?

Pick a specimen with bright, clear eyes. The crocodilian has a second eyelid under his outer eyelid. This second lid is clearly transparent, protects the eyes when the owner is under water. On land, these eyelids should be open except, of course, if the animal is asleep.

Pick a meaty specimen — not bulging necessarily, but well padded, with a straight back. Make sure he has a clear skin and no fungus problem. Select an active specimen, one that wiggles, grunts and nips when you pick him up. If he's under a foot long, the bare hand should do—over a foot, a glove or net should be used. (Don't worry about the grunting — it's quite normal.)

To hold an alligator properly, hold the neck between thumb and forefinger, with the other three fingers around the body.

Now that you have your own personal croc, where's he going to stay?

Some owners like to brag that their pet has the run of the house but the sensible thing is an oversize tank, since a healthy, well-fed crocodilian will grow rapidly. Dealers recommend a ten-gallon tank as a minimum; a long, low, twenty or thirty gallon aquarium is a better investment for the future. Good size for a 12-inch or less specimen is a twenty gallon tank, 12 x 30 x 12 inches high.

For sanitary purposes, the tank should be high enough above the floor for quick and simple draining or siphoning. This simplifies cleaning, which should be done regularly, at least every tenth feeding.

What goes in the tank?

Let's consider the crocodilian's wants. Number one would be warm, clear water. Cold kills the tropical caiman, cool water numbs him—tepid water is what he needs. A 40-watt overhead aquarium light (incandescent, not fluorescent) is a good way to provide both light and warm air over the water.

Tropical creatures are used to about 12 hours a day of bright light, with slightly cooler but not chilly nights. Reliable, inexpensive heating units and clock switches are available which will enable the owner to have light and 90-degree F. in the

In holding the baby caiman or alligator, grip behind jaws with thumb and forefinger and place other three fingers around body, as at top. For feeding, rest the neck in the crotch of the first and second fingers (bottom sketch) which gently restrains the pet.

daytime, 80-degree F. without light at night, automatically. Thermostats are wonderful things! Incidentally, the room the tank is in should never grow cooler than 60 degrees F.

Why is the light so important? Crocodilians in the wild and in captivity sun bathe for hours on end; in fact it has been estimated that they spend 95 percent of their time without moving a muscle, although this is probably an exaggeration.

This sun bathing isn't just to acquire a tan. If you'll notice, the crocodilian's limbs are often stretched out with feet palms up, digits spread wide to obtain maximum exposure to sunlight and air. The light and air are natural inhibitors of bacteria, algae and fungus.

Very high temperatures or too much light are not good for your pet.

Sun lamps or ultra-violet lamps can compensate for the lack of direct sunlight, but can do great harm if used too closely or for excessive periods of time. The pet owner is better off to avoid them unless thoroughly familiar with their use.

Temperatures of 100 degrees F. or more can be fatal to most reptiles. For crocodilians, 80 to 90 degrees F. is ideal; at 65-75 degrees, most specimens refuse to feed or feed indifferently, and become subject to respiratory or intestinal infection, while growth slows greatly.

Crocodilian as a Pet

Your pet will need a "haul-out" spot — a dry place where he can leave the water to sun. There should be sufficient water for him to submerge with an inch or two to spare, and the "dry land" area should take up about one-quarter or one-third of the tank. A rock is perhaps the most practical crawl-out spot, since wood is apt to soak and foul. A sloping rock is desirable but not essential, since crocodilians are far more agile climbers than turtles. Be sure the croc can get completely out of the water; this lessens the danger of fungus infection.

The creature needs warmth, light, a dry place —and shade. Arrange the tank so that your pet can get out of the light if he so desires. Small potted plants at the end of the tank away from the light will be helpful here.

What does a crocodilian eat? His diet is exclusively animal but of wide range. In the wild, it begins with insects, spiders, crustaceans, fish, turtles, reptiles, birds, and works up to mammals such as dogs, deer, or cattle as the animal increases in size and strength. In brief, you might say that the alligator eats anything that comes along — save man.

In captivity, feeding presents a problem at first.

Feeding dishes can be put into the crocodilian's tank, but hand feeding is usually necessary. Unfortunately, most South American alligators do not feed voluntarily and must be coaxed.

The creature is snappish, although his small teeth are hardly capable of breaking the skin. But this can be an advantage — a morsel of food can be placed in the mouth while it is open, to be promptly swallowed. Best method of holding them for such feeding is to rest the neck in the crotch of the first and second fingers, which provides restraint without undue irritation.

Essential for such feeding is a forceps — two prongs of metal or wood, about 12 inches long, tapering to a blunt point, fastened at the base to a block to give the necessary spring action. A rubber casing for the feeding end is advisable to protect the mouth of your pet.

This method of feeding by forceps is recommended because it seems to stimulate the crocodilian to eat better and because it leaves no excess food about to foul up the aquarium.

A specimen reluctant to open his mouth can be induced to do so by tapping the tip of his snout lightly with a finger. Or, a sluggish specimen can be persuaded to have some dinner by passing the food morsel over his nostrils.

Crocodilians will eat as well out of water as they will in water. Basic foods for these carnivorous creatures are raw meat and raw fish. Diet

A good-sized 20-gallon tank gives your pet room to move about, provides for future growth. A 40-watt light provides both light and warm air. A rock provides a good spot for sunning, while small potted plants at the opposite end of the tank, as shown, provide a shady spot where the creature can get out of the light if he so desires.

should be varied as often as possible with large insects, crawfish, frogs, small mice, mollusks. Entire animals should be offered when possible — for example, a small fish or a piece of whole fish is better than a chunk of clear fish meat. The former have a calcium and vitamin content lacking in clear muscle tissue, and aid in growth. Your pet will make his preferences known.

Live goldfish or bait minnows are relished.

Young crocs need certain vitamins, especially D, in abundance. Calcium requirements may be met by the use of bone meal and Vitamin D in the form of cod liver oil. Bite-size morsels of meat can be dipped in cod liver oil and sprinkled with bone meat; the oil odor stimulates your pet's appetite. Your pet will also find many of the commercial dog and cat foods appetizing, although they are not too convenient to feed.

What about the rugged individual who just won't eat? After the first two weeks, you'll have to encourage him firmly. Pry open his jaws by pressing close to the point where they hinge to the skull; hold them open with a small stick. Then ease in a small strip of raw fish or lean raw beef or liver about one third the size of the 'gator's mouth. Force it gently but firmly through the flap which separates the mouth from the gullet, using the eraser end of a pencil.

One or two force-feedings should do the trick.

As a rule, a small individual will eat daily and thrive. Or, if he's fed every third day he'll still do all right. The crocodilian can be fed as often as he will eat — and there's no such thing as overfeeding. When he's had enough he'll stop.

Crocodilian as a Pet

Some authorities advise feeding them no more than twice a week, since their rate of food assimilation is slower than in mammals and birds.

Occasionally many reptiles undergo a period of fasting. This is not abnormal but if it occurs as the result of too low temperature it hinders normal development.

Have you got a boy or a girl 'gator? It's virtually impossible to tell; the only fairly certain method of telling sex in the young is by structure of scales around the vent. In the male, these scales are large and flat — in the female, quite small and beadlike.

In any event, you'll not be apt to set up your own baby 'gator business, since mating doesn't take place until the saurians are at least six years old (some naturalists say ten.)

Mating takes place only under favorable captive conditions in any case, usually in outdoor enclosures.

In regard to disease, it is well to remember that many species of crocodilians live continuously or part-time in salt or slightly salty water. Since salt has a slightly antiseptic effect, a tablespoonful of rock, kosher or specially-prepared aquarium salt per gallon of water may be placed in the tank. (Table salt clouds the water.)

Vitamin deficiency manifests itself most clearly among crocodilians in poor development of teeth, which tend to grow outward at an angle instead of vertically as is normal. Bones of the lower jaw and snout will have a flexibility entirely abnormal. Avoid these symptoms by vitamin supplementation of diet and by maintaining high enough temperatures to prevent prolonged fasting.

Fortunately, the pet owner will rarely encounter any of the external and internal parasites that

Although the 'gator is a mild-mannered cuss, once roused he is dangerous. That's why 'gator wrestlers can't afford to lose a fall.

Northern zoos get surprising numbers of saurians each year, for free. This is because a good-sized crocodilian is apt to upset all your living room furniture and make callers a bit jumpy too.

bother wild crocodilians, since a young specimen has had no opportunity to acquire parasites.

You'll find it interesting to measure and weigh your pet when first you buy him and keep a record of his growth. In captivity, a foot a year seems to be the generally accepted standard. (A well-fed gator should literally bulge with fat in the tail, right behind the rear legs.)

Alligators have individual personalities; it is possible you'll become quite attached to yours. But the day will come when you must realize that a 12-foot, 600-pound brute is too big to have around the living room. Most owners begin to have doubts when their pet gets to be a healthy two or three feet.

The humane thing is to present your specimen to the nearest zoo. Obviously, if released in Northern states he'd be apt to freeze in winter. In summer, he would be equally out of place.

As a conversation piece, your South American alligator has his points; and for anyone who prides himself on having a way with animals, here is the ultimate challenge.

If you intend to raise alligators in wholesale lots, be sure of one thing — a large and constant supply of fish. Most operators feed them once a week most of the year, not at all in the winter. The St. Augustine Alligator Farm specimens are the world's fattest — they dine each and every day!

The Alligator Farms

UST WHAT IS A FARM? Says the dictionary: "A piece of land on which crops or animals are raised." Thus you might say that every roadside stand along Florida's highways with a couple of alligators penned out back for visitors to see is an alligator farm.

Or, in another sense of the word, taking a farm to be a place where a large harvest was obtained each fall you might say that Florida had few 'gator farms — or none — for the systematic raising of hundreds of baby alligators as a meat and hide crop hasn't yet begun here (though experiments in that direction are under way.)

Fortunately, the happy vacationer isn't too concerned with definitions. He just wants to have a look at some alligators. He won't find too many up in North Florida. But Central and South Florida have alligators they haven't even used!

Obviously, it would be impossible to list all the many places where you can see alligators. So we'll just mention a few of the main attractions which, in their way, embody this interesting bit of Florida show business. Let's start with the granddaddy of them all.

ST. AUGUSTINE ALLIGATOR FARM: This is the big, big one, boasting acres of live suitcases, advertising more than 6,000 saurians great and small. You'll find it in a tropical setting on Route A1A, about two miles south of St. Augustine, only a few hundred feet from the Atlantic Ocean.

Each year more than a quarter million tourists visit the farm, owned and operated by F. Charles Usina and W. I. Drysdale, native Floridians.

But they are not the first alligator farmers. Joseph "Alligator Joe" Campbell of Jacksonville, Fla., earned that distinction in 1891 when he established his Florida Alligator Farm on what is now the site of the Prudential's modern skyscraper office building in South Jacksonville.

A second Florida farm was started in 1893 by George T. Reddington and Felix Fire of St. Augustine, on Anastasia Island near that city.

"Used to be a train ran from St. Augustine to St. Augustine Beach," Usina recalls. "Reddington was the conductor, Fire was the fireman. They'd pick up alligators that got on the tracks, and put them in an old bathhouse out on the beach. Tourists kept bothering them to see the alligators, so they started charging a quarter. Then they built their first farm out at the end of the train tracks, on the beach."

Usina and Drysdale got into the business in a less logical way. For years, they were partners in a St. Augustine haberdashery — Charlesdale, Inc. But both were keen on hunting, fishing and the outdoors. When the Reddington-Fire alligator farm was put up for sale in 1937, it seemed logical to them to swap suits, shirts and socks for saurians. By combining the collections of Campbell, Reddington and Fire, they began one of the world's largest and oldest assortments of 'gators.

The Alligator Farms

Looking around the spacious pens, one thing is obvious; these are the fattest alligators anywhere, anytime. Their jowls fairly bulge; their plated midriffs look like barrels as they lie sluggish in the sun, and the visitor wonders how they can even stir their bulk.

Food, of course, is the answer. Most alligators in captivity get one or two meals a week (except for winter when they get none at all.) But these massive suitcases chow down each and every day —and they look it! This planned overfeeding keeps the stock from devouring one another.

The alligator in captivity is no show-off; mostly, he just lies there. Even so, Usina and Drysdale over the years have found him fascinating to everyone. Each year, the farm receives letters in French, German, Spanish, Italian, Portugese and Greek as well as plain English, asking for information and photos.

For several years, a maharajah from India has been corresponding with the farm, getting minute details on how to operate his own saurian ranch in his country!

The alligator is an ideal candidate for captivity; all he asks is that the chow keeps coming,

Nothing spells "FLORIDA" to the visitor like the Seminole Indians and the alligator. When the two get together, as above, in a wrestling match at Musa Isle in Miami, the combination is an ideal tourist attraction.

and room is provided to doze in the sun while awaiting the next meal.

Usina and Drysdale say, after years of observation, that there is no such creature as a trained alligator. The dime-sized brain operates "by instinct only," they argue.

A farm operator must consider the cannibalistic tendencies of his charges. Planned overfeeding of the 6,000 specimens with tons of raw fish and meat avoids and self-decimation of the stock.

Alligators are gregarious; the specimens of the Campbell, Fire and Reddington collections have lived together more than 50 years and seem to recognize themselves as a group. They fight among themselves, but not to the death. But when a strange alligator is brought in from the wilds, the "members of the club" are apt to charge him.

ARKANSAS ALLIGATOR FARM: One of the nation's first alligator farms was started in 1894,

The alligator farm at Nature's Giant Fish Bowl, Homosassa Springs, is one of Florida's most unusual. As the photo above indicates, these fortunate saurians enjoy spacious natural surroundings — their home is simply a fenced-in section of the Homosassa River itself.

This dramatic sculptured scene of a Seminole about to grapple with a huge alligator makes an effective front entrance display at Okalee Indian Village near Dania on Florida's East Coast. Attraction features only deep water alligator wrestling on view in the country as far as can be determined.

The Alligator Farms

the year after the Reddington-Fire operation began. This is the Arkansas Alligator Farm, still going strong at Hot Springs National Park. Manager L. F. Stauler reports that about 40,000 visitors a year have a look at the farm's 125 alligators of all sizes, along with assorted monkeys, turtles, ground hogs and foxes.

From April 15 to the middle of October, the Arkansas alligators live outdoors; then, when things turn cool, they're herded into a large building with a pool in the center. Here, as in most farms, they are not fed during the winter.

ROSS ALLEN'S REPTILE INSTITUTE: In the center of Florida at Silver Springs, just outside Ocala. Remarkable for two things — one of the country's finest collection of crocodilia, 14 different species of alligators, caimans, crocodiles and gavials; and Ross Allen himself.

Entering the Institute's pioneer cabin, you'll find an unusual 'gator souvenir—skulls of all sizes. Just the thing to send a maiden aunt from Florida! Out on the grounds in concrete pits, carefully screened with wire and shaded from the sun, you'll see the fruit of Allen's 29 expeditions to Latin America.

Here, for instance, are five grayish Cuban crocodiles, found only in the swamps of Cuba and almost extinct. They're as vicious as they are scarce, can jump almost three feet straight up in the air!

Here's a black caiman, protected by Florida law because he looks so much like the alligator. Here are his relatives — the smooth-fronted caiman with his curious head, the dwarf caiman, the spectacled caiman.

Here's an African sharp-nosed crocodile, and in the next pit an Indian gavial with a long, slender snout ideal for catching fish.

Nearby are Allen's "naturalistic" alligator corrals; pools surrounded by aquatic vegetation are linked by ditches which allows the water to circulate.

One of the more colorful inhabitants was Old Cannibal. This 12-footer was captured by Allen

An old Seminole custom. Here's an alligator wrestling trick that makes the customers gasp — the young brave tucks his chin over the alligator's lower jaw and removes his hands from the reptile's snout. A nice trick—but be sure you don't lose that jaw hold!

The Alligator Farms

near Webster, Florida, after ranchers there said the big 'gator was killing their cattle.

Brought to the Institute and put in a pen with 13 smaller animals for company, Old Cannibal seemed content enough — until one night he went on a rampage and killed the others. (This is not uncommon where a large specimen is placed with several smaller ones.)

Old Cannibal was just plain mean. Thus Institute workers were startled one morning to find that a large female 'gator had come out of the nearby swamp, made her way through or under the fence and was sharing Cannibal's bed and board!

The couple lived happily ever after, producing a number of litters prior to the male's death in 1960.

"Alligators are individualists," says Allen. "Some will attack, some won't. You can't make rules for animals."

Allen's family came to Winter Haven, Florida, in 1924, from Ohio. At 16, Ross had already developed a keen interest in wild things and began collecting snakes. In the Florida wilderness, teeming with alligators and snakes, wildcats, deer, coon, fox and turkey, he found an ideal hunting ground. His hobbies of swimming and taxidermy fitted the picture; in 1929 he moved into a small shack in a cypress swamp at Silver Springs, installed a rattler and a couple of alligators. He meant to be a taxidermist but had so many visitors

Indian alligator trap. This innocent-looking assortment of stakes alongside the Weekiwachee River leads into an S-curve which wedges food-seeking alligator in tight when he tries to back out. (See diagram.) No longer in use by Seminoles, who find the supermarket simpler.

The Alligator Farms

he began charging 10 cents admission and another Florida alligator farm was born!

Over the years, Allen and his alligators have appeared in over two dozen Grantland Rice Sportlights films and many news shorts, while he has doubled or acted in a number of movies.

The visitor to the Institute gets a remarkable look at an impressive collection of creatures, with lecture tours each hour on the hour. On view are all sorts of 'gators, crocodiles and caimans, plus snakes, turtles, panthers, black bears, flamingoes, raccoons—in short, just about all of Florida's wild life. Thrilling climax of the lecture tour—a for-real demonstration of the "milking" of a venomous snake. Also interesting: A Seminole Indian village.

Famed for his work in supplying anti-venom for the armed forces during World War II, Allen has been bitten 10 times by poisonous snakes and lived; and only a very cool head has kept him intact after years of handling alligators.

An example of this iron self-control came during the filming of the 'gator-catching sequence for a movie some years ago.

Allen was in a cypress swamp pool, the cameras grinding away as he demonstrated his method of capturing a wild alligator with Old Cannibal as "model." As usual, he leaped upon the alligator from behind, clamped a scissors hold around the body with his legs and held the snout shut with his hands. There was a brief but violent struggle as he hung on — then he worked the 'gator to the bank and up onto the grass.

As he began to truss up the jaws, the little slip that can be deadly occurred. Quicker than thought, Old Cannibal freed his snout and clamped down on Allen's hand.

It's customary for celebrities to have their pictures taken with the local attractions — be it bullfighting or alligator wrestling. Above, the late Gary Cooper gingerly holds the tail of a husky alligator at the Reptile Institute at Silver Springs, where many movies and newsreels have been filmed. Alligator looks a bit bored with it all.

The cameramen were so startled they froze—probably the best thing they could have done, since any sudden move might have excited the brute. Allen, too, held motionless, knowing that when an alligator makes up its foggy mind to kill, it seeks to dismember.

Despite pain and loss of blood, Allen held his position. His big gamble: He hoped that if he did not struggle the alligator might open its jaws for another bite. Minutes dragged by as he stared at Old Cannibal's eyes; at last he felt the jaw muscles relax a bit and the jaws opened slightly. He snatched out his hand, leaped backward and the danger was past — just another close one for this nerveless naturalist.

OWEN GODWIN'S GATORLAND: Four miles north of Kissimmee on U.S. 27-92. Big attraction here for fourteen years was an enormous gray log with wicked yellowish eyes. The log went by the name of Old Bonecrusher. Fourteen feet three inches long, weighing 1080 pounds, this huge crocodile was taken alive off Key Largo in a shark net in the mid-fifties. He was believed to be the world's largest captive croc when he died in 1970.

You'd think being the only crocodile in a herd of 50 alligators at Homosassa Springs would make him nervous — but not this fellow! Above, center, he enjoys the company of two alligators. If another croc is put in the river enclosure they fight; but the 'gators and the regular tenant get along fine.

The Alligator Farms

The stocky, blue-eyed owner, born and raised at Rattlesnake Hammock on the Kissimmee River nearby, opened his attraction in 1950 after a profitable fling at the restaurant business. Gatorland is something he's always wanted. He has a 20-acre operation.

"Certainly they'll mate," he says, pointing out that all they need is a bit of privacy.

There is a heavy stand of tall Australian pines set back from the lakeside. Here in the dappled shade, carpeted with brown pine needles, the females of Godwin's 107-head herd nest in summer. Spotted here and there are inconspicuous mounds about two feet high by five feet wide. Lying within ten or fifteen feet of these mounds are female alligators, apparently dozing. But when man comes near, explosive hisses arise, warning all comers to keep their distance.

Under the pine needle mounds there is a dark, warm, moist compost of leaves and twigs, covering many long white eggs — not as large in circumference as a hen's egg, but longer, equally rounded on each end.

By fall, each nest will average perhaps 40 small saurians, assuming they don't get eaten first by predators or a larger alligator.

It doesn't disturb an alligator when the nest is moved. Godwin waits until the egg-laying is finished, then moves the nests closer to his zoo area — the better to be on hand and catch the young when they hatch and make their break for the water.

Like all 'gator men, Godwin has a healthy respect for the saurian: "These people that say alligators are harmless, don't know what they're talking about." Some just happen to be meaner than others, he says.

WEEKIWACHEE SPRINGS: While this attraction on U.S. 19, some 60 miles north of St. Petersburg, is chiefly noted for its mermaid shows,

Lester (left) and Bill Piper look over some of their Everglades Wonder Gardens stock. The two veteran outdoorsmen captured many of these specimens themselves. Farm has probably the nation's finest collection of crocodiles.

The Alligator Farms

it offers an interesting wildlife display along the crystal-clear Weekiwachee River. Part of this display is a pen of alligators on the river bank, in very clear view—a fact which enabled former Springs zoologist John Hamlet to obtain facts on the alligator's mating ritual seldom recorded.

Another unique exhibit is an Indian alligator trap, an exact replica made and installed by Hamlet from a sketch drawn by an aged redskin who had heard it described by his elders.

Modern-day Seminoles have lost many such devices from olden times, the need no longer being there.

HOMOSASSA SPRINGS: Unique to the attraction is the manner in which the herd of 50 alligators (and 2 lonesome crocodiles) are fed, three times daily. A mullet is attached to a clothespin on a long trolley line that stretches across the 'gator lagoon. An attendant pulls the line and the mullet goes riding out over the massed alligators until—with unbelievable speed—saurians leap up out of the water and gobble up the fish. Mullet lowered on a string produces the same result.

Also on view at the springs: Otters, sea lions, a genuine hippo, a deer park, an aviary and an orchid garden, all in most attractive natural surroundings.

Located 80 miles north of the Tampa-St. Petersburg area on U.S. 19, this huge, bowl-shaped spring was for many years known as Nature's Giant Fish Bowl. In its crystal-clear waters, 72 degrees year-round, as many as 34 varieties of fresh and salt water fish can be seen.

The 'gator herd gets along fairly well, since plenty of food is available. Once a rogue 'gator made trouble, however. He was tied up and his two tusk teeth—several inches long—were pulled.

After that he behaved himself, almost as if he knew he couldn't bite the way he used to!

HOMOSASSA SPRINGS, Fla. . . . . Visitors to Homosassa Springs enjoy alligator feedings at the Gator Lagoon where more than 50 alligators and crocodiles live in a natural state. 'Gators jump from the water to take fish on a string from attendants. And you can feed the 'gators their favorite snack—marshmallows!

The Alligator Farms

He points over the fence and there is seven-foot Buddy himself — big and peaceable, keeping his mouth shut on the river bank.

When mating season comes, the Fish Bowl alligators pair off and lay eggs in nests along the river bank. Since Meybem doesn't want to bother raising alligators, he simply collects the eggs (when it's safe to do so) and sends them over to Ross Allen's Reptile Institute at Silver Springs, where they're hatched out. An average collection, 150 eggs.

TRANS-WORLD WILDLIFE FARMS: This is Mississippi's major alligator center, located on U.S. 90 just 7 miles west of Bay St. Louis, Miss. Owner C. A. Boal, starting this as a hobby back in July, 1951, has seen it grow into a major operation over the past decade.

On 22 acres of land containing considerable lake area, he has about 100 alligators in natural they and the garfish also add to the alligator diet. This situation is controlled since the two lakes are fenced apart — otherwise the garfish and turtle population would dwindle rapidly.

Owner Boal has been successful in his breed-surroundings, with nesting space along the lakeside. His biggest specimen (most of his saurians were obtained from Florida) runs 12 feet 4 inches long.

Trans-World has a unique feature — a floating food supply. Boal has a lakeful of 30,000 turtles, give or take a turtle, all sizes from dinner-plate to pocket-watch. The lake also teems with another favorite snack of saurians, the predatory garfish. This turtle lake is a sight indeed, probably unequalled in the world, for it is studded with cruising hardshells, their curious heads sticking straight up like a forest of periscopes!

Live cargo. Ross Allen and his three husky sons — Robert, Tom and John — boat some unwilling passengers taken from swamp waters. Note careful manner in which snout is secured by noose around neck. This prevents alligator from clawing off nose rope, which could be disastrous.

The Alligator Farms

Trans-World sells the turtles as souvenirs; but ing operation here; this is one of the nation's most likely mass farm projects.

An outstanding example is C. C. McClung's Snake Farm, LaPlace, Louisiana, which sells more than 5,000 baby alligators a year, shipping to all parts of the world.

A breeder's permit allows the farm to raise, sell and keep in captivity any amount of alligators at one time.

"I have more than 100 breeders that lay their eggs in the breeding pen," says McClung. "I collect the eggs each day and place them in large tubs of leaves and decaying vegetation to hatch."

His rates on Alligator Mississipiensis by mail run from $4 for a baby to $6 for a 2-footer, $100 for a 6-footer, $800 for a 10-footer, and $1000 and up for any specimen over 10 feet.

EVERGLADES WONDER GARDENS: Operated by Bill and Lester Piper since 1938, this well-known attraction is located on the Tamiami Trail (U. S. 41) 23 miles south of Fort Myers. This is the home of big ones. The Piper brothers have collections of the biggest alligators and crocodiles you'll see anywhere.

They're particularly proud of their crocodile pool. And of a letter from W. M. Mann, Smithsonian Institution, who wrote after a visit: "I still stay aghast at the thought of your 32 crocodiles in one enclosure."

"Dynamite" is king of the pool, and a fantastic sight he is, too, with his huge grayish armored body stretching 14 feet and some inches. (The Pipers don't know exactly how long he is, and nobody has volunteered to measure. However, to this observer he was very nearly the same size as Owen Godwin's huge 14-foot 3-inch crocodile, "Old Bonecrusher.")

In a separate pen at the side is "Big Joe" a bad actor who killed seven other crocodiles over a period of a few months about 1949. He's a 12-footer — and you'll find two other 12-footers off by themselves on the other side of the main tank, also bad actors. The alligator pool is full of big ones too, scores of them, 10, 12, 14 feet long, many caught by the Pipers themselves in the nearby Imperial River.

George Weymouth, guide at the Gardens, points out differences between two crocodilians:

"Alligators don't mind piling up on each other," he says. "But the crocodiles seem to want their own corners; they'll fight newcomers where alligators won't. 'Gators do their fighting at mating season; crocs seem to bicker all year round."

A pen for small specimens — 4-5 feet long — offers an excellent chance to compare the Nile Crocodile, American Crocodile, Spectacled Caiman and American Alligator; 40 specimens of all four types are mixed here.

Once you see the Nile croc's yellowish skin and thicker snout, you could never again mistake him for the American brand.

Bill and Lester Piper, farm boys from Southern Ohio, grew up fishing and hunting. They first saw Florida when their parents came here during

These lucky beasts have one of the finest homes in Florida — the beautiful Homosassa River just below Nature's Fish Bowl. Water temperature of 74 degrees keeps them warm in winter.

The Alligator Farms

the 1910 land boom; their late father, Joseph D. Piper, was a St. Petersburg city fireman for a time. In 1931, driving around the state, they liked the wilderness look of Bonita Springs on the edge of the Everglades and settled down;

They're jealous of their carefully-developed collection of American crocodiles from the nearby Keys:

"We've parted with only two of them," says Bill. "One to Ross Allen and one to the U.S. Army. During World War II they wanted one to train boys for jungle survival — teach 'em to recognize a crocodile. We sent one up to a big airfield, never did get him back." It would be most interesting to know the fate of that patriotic crocodile that went off to the wars some 20 years ago!

MUSA ISLE SEMINOLE INDIAN VILLAGE: Here the gators and the Indians, both symbols of primitive Florida, are about as close to civilization as they can get — at NW 25th Ave. and 16th Street in Miami. G. L. Stacey of the Village says it was set up on the north fork of the Miami River in 1922, has been owned and operated by the same family ever since.

What makes the Village different is the fact that nine Seminole families make their home there. Visitors can see, on a guided tour, all their ways of life as the Seminoles go about their normal routine around the palm-thatched "chickee" huts.

There's work for the braves while the women sew their colorful skirts and shirts — 'gator wrestling.

"Frequency of our wrestling shows depends on the season," says Stacey. "Generally they start at 10:30 a.m., the last at 5 p.m., spaced 45 minutes to an hour apart."

In addition to about 100 alligators, the largest running 12 feet, the Village has 11 crocodiles, the two largest being 10 feet.

For the photographer, there's color aplenty—beautiful parrots, macaws, flamingos; Seminoles in flaming native costume, all amid a tropical setting of palms, bamboo and native flora.

OKALEE INDIAN VILLAGE (Arts and Craft Center): Newest of these attractions and certainly one of the most unusual, it is located 20 miles north of Miami on State Road 7 (U.S. 441) near Dania, Hollywood and Fort Lauderdale on Florida's East Coast. Two things make it different. Developed gradually, the village has been in operation only about a year at the time of this writing. Direct management of the project is in the hands of the board of directors of the Seminole Tribe.

They borrowed $150,000 from the federal government, constructed a beautiful Arts and Crafts center plus a genuine Seminole village and took out after the wily tourist. The village broke even during its first year of operation — even though

old timers in Florida show biz say it takes three to five years for a new attraction to begin paying. Profits, of course, will be shared by members of the tribal corporation, who inhabit the Dania Reservation.

A second feature that makes Okalee Indian Village different is for-real deep water alligator wrestling by the braves — and we mean brave. This is the only place in the U.S.A. (and the world for that matter) where you can see this version of the native Floridian sport, if you can call it that.

And how the tourist cameras click and whirr when a husky young Seminole plunges into the same pool with a big seven-foot alligator, grapples with the beast underwater, hauls him to the surface in a welter of foam and pilots him ashore! Here the Indian climaxes the performance by wrestling his captive over on his back, whereupon the animal promptly passes out — a thing which never ceases to amaze the visitor.

The 14-acre village, one reviewer recently noted, "is being operated on a high plane, featuring cleanliness, neatness, authenticity, and the 20th century need — free parking . . . Everything has been designed for today's tourist . . . authentic Seminole-made souvenirs." The Okalee village "far surpasses any of the Seminole camps open to the public in south Florida," Max Huhn reported in The Christian Science Monitor.

Winding canals border 20 thatched-roof chickees; a guide leads a tour where the visitor will see Seminoles at traditional tasks such as basket weaving, leather work, carving, corn-grinding in wooden mortars, hewing out cypress log canoes. There's no shortage of talent; about one-third of Florida's 1,100 Seminoles — give or take a Seminole — live on the Dania Reservation.

On certain days they stage some of their ritual dances. But since the Seminole traditional dances are slow, shuffling and not spectacular, the tribe is training the young ones to do various Sioux and Cherokee dances that look more like what the tourist thinks an Indian dance should be! (At Okalee, the paleface is always right.)

Interesting point: The Dania Seminoles are devout Christians. Therefore — unlike many white businessmen — they refuse to open their attraction on Sunday, a prime day for business. Nor is the village open at night.

"The village," says Frank W. Long, business management adviser, "is primarily educational in that it gives the public a wealth of information about the Seminoles, past and present."

When you see that sight of sights — an unarmed Indian, grappling with one of nature's most dangerous, powerful brutes — you'll agree that the Okalee Indian Village is, indeed, educational!

The Alligator Farms

This is a textbook Alligator Farm complete with the "oldest, largest, ugliest 'gator in captivity". The owners, camping enthusiasts, welcome families with children who enjoy watching the beasts from a close-up but safe vantage point.

GATORLAND: This well kept menagerie of Florida wildlife, located two miles north of St. Augustine on US 1, was established during the Florida financial famine of 1930 and has been operated since that time. In addition to several hundred saurians, an excellent sampling of Florida's more common wildlife is exhibited under meticulous conditions. There is a continuous demonstration of techniques involved in capturing and handling alligators. While you are here, be sure to ask for the amiable Jim Martin, the ranch foreman, and he will provide you with a simple, down-to-earth, backwoods dissertation on the habits and habitats of the renown Florida 'gator. There is limited free over-night parking for self-contained campers. Ray and Dorothy Ettel, the owners, are both avid campers and can entertain you for hours with their experiences in the great outdoors.

"Biggest In The World". That's a challenge that has always fascinated men no matter what the subject.

The Big Ones

INCE BEFORE THE TROJAN HORSE or the Great Wall of China, as long ago as the Pyramids or the Cardiff Giant, man has been fascinated by sheer bulk. In no case is this more true than that of the crocodilians. But here, man has worked against himself.

Around 1791, William Bartram, the Quaker naturalist, traveled through Florida and reported big ones galore — some 20 feet in length. Although most people, describing a king-size specimen of anything from fish to alligator, will add on a few feet or inches to improve the story, Bartram quite likely was not far off.

Consider: An alligator has no natural enemies, aside from another alligator bigger than he is. Man had not yet appeared on the scene. The land teemed with food. What was to stop his steady growth, to become the "very large and terrible creature" described by Bartram?

Just how big can the crocodilians get?

Back in the Age of Dinosaurs, a 45-foot crocodile roamed around. In modern times, some writers speak loosely of 30-foot gavials. But the hard, cold figures of the record books—meaning that somebody with a tape measure actually laid the critter out and checked him stem to stern — are not so generous. The top length ever recorded among the crocodilians was 23 feet, attained by an American crocodile and one from the Orinoco Basin.

Next under the wire comes a prodigious Indian Gavial which got to be 21 feet, 6 inches long. The

How big an alligator was this? Answer — 12 feet. This big one was killed in a fight with another alligator at McClung's Snake Farm, LaPlace, La.

The Big Ones

biggest salt water crocodile went 20 feet. And, of course, the all-time giant American Alligator was a 19-foot, 2-inch specimen shot by the father of the noted Louisiana naturalist, E. A. McIlhenny. After that they taper down, the record specimens, to little fellows of 15 and 16 feet or so.

Are there bigger specimens than these? Could be. You'll hear some stories about alligators that swam alongside of somebody's 20-foot boat and matched it foot for foot. Or tracks the size of a dinner-plate. But there's a big difficulty. To have rabbit stew you have to catch the rabbit — and it's difficult to measure a monster that doesn't want to be measured.

"The largest alligator I ever measured was from Lake Apopka, killed by a hunter," says Ross Allen. "The 'gator measured 16 feet 2 inches." Allen's "Big George," pride of the Institute, went 14 feet, 7 inches, may well have been the largest specimen in captivity. Most other alligator farms will claim at least a 12-footer. Sign painters will add a foot or two just to help out. No tourist yet has turned up with a tape measure and the desire to check up on a big specimen.

Old Bonecrusher, 14-feet 3-inch whopper at Godwin's Gatorland, seems to have been top crocodile in captivity.

Big ones are still around, however. During the 1959-60 season, one hunting permit holder reported killing a granddaddy saurian 17 feet long. If the hunter could have taken him alive (a neat trick) he could have realized ten times the profit.

In May, 1957, the U. S. Fish and Wildlife Service, Washington, D. C., reported that 12 feet is now regarded near the alligator maximum, although 15-footers were run-of-the-swamp a century ago, and 14-footers not uncommon 50 years ago. The check was made after a 13½ foot alligator was captured at the Delta National Wildlife Refuge in Louisiana, biggest ever taken there.

Still, if what this country needs is a good 20-foot alligator, we may see the big ones back in another 50 years or so. For places like the St. Augustine Alligator Farm have specimens galore that just eat and sleep, eat and sleep, year after year. It seems inevitable that these worthies, safe from hunters, will ultimately grow their way into glory.

The fact is that an alligator's age and rate of growth are both highly undecided questions.

F. Charles Usina and W. I. Drysdale, co-owners of the St. Augustine Alligator Farm, point out that an alligator's age cannot be judged from his size. Comparing their growth charts with those kept by the late Raymond Ditmars of the Bronx Zoo, those of E. A. McIlhenny of Avery Island, Louisiana, and charts prepared by the first Florida alligator farmer, Joseph Campbell, they have found no agreement.

Usina and Drysdale point out that alligators

How big can an alligator get around the middle? When he's fed to capacity there's almost no limit, as witness these whopping saurians posing for a Christmas scene with a veteran guide at the noted St. Augustine Alligator Farm.

The Big Ones

in the past have far outlived humans who would study them; far too few wild animals have been tagged to give accurate figures on their growth in the natural state.

Stronger alligators grow faster, the farm operators point out, simply because the ones that get the most food at first, grow larger and thus take more and more food from the smaller ones. (Despite his vast appetite, an alligator can live from a month to a year without food. Some say two years.)

Estimates of growth rate vary widely — from an inch to a foot per year. A specimen named Whitey was checked carefully at the Reptile Institute by Ross Allen for almost 20 years. Captured when he was just under two feet long and weighing only a few pounds, Whitey ten years later

was almost five feet long and weighing 30 pounds. Five years after that, he had added another foot in length, weighed about 100 pounds. When 30 years old, he was slightly over seven feet long, weighed 225 pounds.

Yet one popular reference booklet declares that "In the wild, a ten-foot male American alligator will attain that length in about the same number of years."

McIlhenny estimated that an alligator, to attain 15 feet in length must live for at least 30 or 40 years.

The goal of alligator farmers, of course, is growth and plenty of it — a foot a year or more. For the present, however, rate of growth remains something of a mystery still to be unraveled by patient research.

Old Cannibal, the meanest 'gator Ross Allen ever had at his Reptile Institute. He killed 13 smaller alligators in one night before being put in solitary confinement.

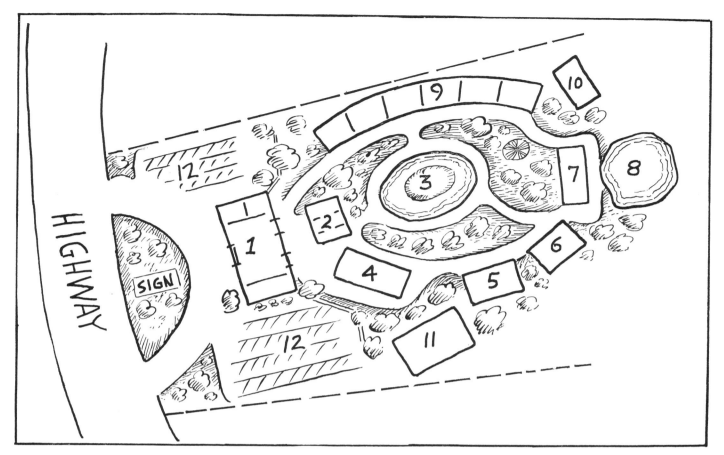

TYPICAL ALLIGATOR FARM LAYOUT — Since frontage on a major highway is expensive, most farms apply the small side of their rectangle to the roadway. Ample parking, of course, is a must, as well as an attractively landscaped entrance area. First impressions are important. Number key: 1. Main building and entrance. Houses gift shop, rest rooms, office, sometimes owners living quarters upstairs. (This is perhaps the best plan, since new business usually requires continuous attention.) 2. Special pens to show off largest specimens. 3. Central pool and pull-out area for as many 'gators as possible. 4. Assortment pen, which should include number of crocodilians, usually small, for purposes of comparison — gavial, caiman, crocodile, alligator. 5, 6, 7, various sizes of 'gators, medium to large — a snake pit may be included here if desired. 8. Natural pool to give visitor a look at alligator in native habitat. If desired, this could be nesting and breeding area too. 9. Cage row for exhibit of various Florida animals such as bobcat, coon, etc. Fully as interesting to many, especially children, as 'gators themselves. 10. Animal food storage house. 11. Storage area, also pen for stock in transit or not suitable for display. (Both 10 and 11 shielded from public by trees, shrubbery.) 12. Parking area. Should include room for expansion. Cement or graveled walkways connect all displays, both walks and pens protected from sun by roofing with exception of central pool, few cages.

'Gator Farm Operation

THINKING OF OPENING an alligator farm yourself? It's a business with a future, certainly. For in Florida, one of the nation's last frontier states with a soaring population and swelling year-round tourist business, there are opportunities waiting the wise businessman.

Yet caution is required. Many a northern investor or retiree has come to Florida, built or bought a motel or attraction with little or no investigation and thought as to site, competition, operating expense and then gone bust.

A. D. Aldrich, director of Florida's Game and Fresh Water Fish Commission, cites the No. 1 requirement for successful entry into the field:

'Gator Farm Operation

"A person planning to operate any kind of wild animal exhibit in Florida should first obtain advice from a competent authority in the field of building and maintaining zoological collections. Such information may be obtained by contacting valid zoological park directors in major cities."

Number two requirement, a look at the competition. As of this writing, 40 possession permits to keep alligators have been issued by the Florida Commission. The majority of these, of course, are simply for the roadside exhibitor who has a few alligators as a sideline curiosity or attraction, the better to sell shells, orange juice, souvenirs or the like.

Assuming you are interested in more of a show for the show's sake, you'll want to visit the major operations mentioned in this book. Take a long, careful look; make up a list and check each operation against it. Try to select the best features of each for your own place.

Essential: If you don't know operating costs — feed, staff salaries, upkeep, utilities, advertising, etc., obtain the advice and estimates of someone who does.

Then ask yourself if you can afford to get through the first year or so while you're establishing yourself. Remember, most of the attractions you've seen have been building up a name and business for 20 years or longer.

The No. 1 consideration in establishing your 'gator farm is location by all means. Here you have several choices. You can be one of a cluster of attractions, as Ross Allen's Reptile Institute is at Silver Springs. Or, you can go it alone.

There are advantages to both ideas. The loner has the business all to himself. The group operator is banking on the likelihood that someone who is initially attracted by some other show may be interested in his too, as well as the person who came to him first. Also, he benefits from the combined advertising package of the group, which is usually more extensive than the lone hand can afford.

We're assuming, of course, that you plan your exhibit in Florida. Although it's likely the competition would be less in, say, Georgia or South Carolina, most people believe in coming where the tourists are; and all the figures say that adds up to Florida.

Just where in Florida? Well, the tourist and the alligator have one thing in common — they both love warmth. In summer this doesn't matter much. But come winter season, there is a difference as much as six degrees between North Florida and Central Florida — and even more when you get down to South Florida. That's a mighty important six degrees; it can spell the difference between people getting outdoors looking for entertainment or staying put. This is why you'll find most of your attractions concentrated in Central and South Florida.

Location on (or very near) one of the main traffic arteries that feed automobiles into the state is another must. You can't be hard to find, for the man headed down state might make a stop-over at your place (if the kids talk him into it) if it's not out of the way — whereas he's not as apt to make a detour off his major highway.

Next question: Will your place be on the edge of the city, or further away? Again, there are pro and con factors to be weighed. Land costs—which we'll consider in a moment—are naturally higher the closer you get to an expanding population center. Yet the closer you are to the family which bases at a motel and sightsees from this base, the better. People will drive 10 or 15 miles to an attraction but are apt to settle for something closer when it becomes a question of 25 or 30 miles, especially if their time is limited. For this reason we're inclined to favor the site a few miles from town, even though initial investment will be more.

Certainly, there will be more competition here; you've got to be willing to compete. But remember you'll be doing it on a constantly expanding market, for Florida tourism is growing as the nation heads into a leisure era which means more vacations, more travel, more sightseeing.

Say that after long and careful analysis, you've decided on your location. It meets zoning requirements of the particular county; it won't become a bog in the rainy season (remember Florida gets over 50 inches of rain a year, 60 percent of this in the summer months.) Does it have some natural shade trees you can take advantage of? Natural pond or stream you can utilize in landscaping and beautifying the property? These things can save you much time and money.

A long-term lease of the land at 1% of value per month, is preferable. After, say five years, you should know if you and the business are compatible. Cost will vary widely, of course, probably in the $10,000-$15,000 bracket. Highway frontage is expensive, naturally. For this reason, you should confine it to your entrance and parking lot, as indicated in our suggested layout sketch. The parking lot, of course, is vital. We'd suggest you plan for at least 50 cars to start, with room for expansion, remembering the great American slogan: If I can't park, I won't stop.

The face you present to the motoring public should be one which invites comparison, one which is different. Remember all the other facades your touring family has seen and come up with something spectacular.

Jungle, Spanish, Old Settler motifs are the most frequently used themes. They're sound — they're what the tourist expects of Florida. But they can be done far better.

This is the era of the big spectacular. Why not be a stand-out? You need a traffic stopper. For example, why not a 45-foot crocodilian in plaster, similar to the dinosaur statues near Rapid City, South Dakota? You've got history to back you up — a creature like this once walked the earth, and is the ancestor of your live exhibits. Give him a pair of red light bulbs for eyes, light

'Gator Farm Operation

him dramatically at night with your attraction's name attached (not too conspiciously) and the results should be most effective.

Remember that thousands of tourist snapshots may be one of your best advertisements. Why not provide a place beside the beast for visitors to stand and be photographed, plus a sign inviting snapshots, and an identification plaque giving a bit of crocodilian history?

Landscaping is important; Florida palms, shrubs, flowers do much to invite the visitor. And never forget that the lady of the house — who makes many of the what-to-see decisions — is very big on cleanliness. A run-down, shabby exterior can drive them away by droves.

Most alligator farms have their gift shop as their entrance, a wise idea. Usually a snack bar is included — and a water fountain is greatly ap-preciated. Rest rooms at one end, office at the other. Gift stock? You'll quickly get an idea of the assortment by checking here and there along the highway. Your alligator farm will usually have extras such as 'gator teeth, bags, key cases.

Speaking of prices — what to charge? Here again, take a look at the field. One school of thought keeps them high, on this theory, this is the only crack I'll ever get at this customer. Another school favors more moderate rates, realizing that a man with a family of four or five kids can't meet too big a tariff.

We know of one alligator farm that simply takes up a collection — with dollar bills from adults, half-dollars from children apparently pre-ferred!

Once the customer has decided to have a look at your attraction, what will he see? Well, most

Feeding time is happy time for always-hungry alligators — even these purposely overfed fatties at St. Augustine Alligator Farm. While most farms feed only once or twice a week, the St. Augustine operation dishes out chow (mostly fish) daily to prevent cannibalism.

'Gator Farm Operation

operators seem to favor an oval layout, as sketched in our drawing of a typical alligator farm. If you have exceptionally large specimens you may want them featured in the place of honor; at the St. Augustine Farm, you'll find the big alligators in individual pens as soon as you step out from the gift shop.

Most farms have a major, centrally-located pool-pen with several dozen specimens. Some, doing it the most economical way, avoid the cement bottom and concrete block side pen (standard) and simply have their animals in a natural pond. This doesn't make for as good visability, however, but does provide a natural setting. Probably the best answer is to have some of each type of pen.

Most farms favor a lower concrete pit, surrounded by a wall about five to six feet high. If a fenced-in wire pen is used, the top should be bent inward or the pen should be covered. A small alligator can scale a six-foot wire fence without much difficulty. Pens are usually divided, half water pool, half crawl-out area where the alligator can sun himself.

A system of running water is recommended between pens. This prevents stagnant, foul water from developing, a condition which is not healthful for the alligators and is likely to repel the visitor by sight and odor.

It is well to plan an "isolation ward" pen for larger alligators who may turn mean and prove a menace to the rest of the herd. (Good examples of these may be seen at Everglades Wonder Gardens.) If you are fortunate enough to have a larger alligator and/or crocodile, these should be displayed to the very best advantage as centerpiece of your exhibit, in individual pens with enough room to move about. Owen Godwin's Gatorland near Kissimmee, Fla. houses "Old Bonecrusher," huge 14-foot 3-inch crocodile, in this manner.

Most alligator farms offer a large variety. In addition to alligators — usually kept in their own size class for survival's sake and a fair chance at food — you'll probably want the usual assortment of sideline animals and birds. Here again you may have to start small and build up. Some exhibits are showing sea cows and porpoises in addition to alligators but these are expensive.

Most will display native Florida animals such as raccoon, 'possum, fox, snakes, squirrels, bob cats — and a few pink flamingos and peacocks for decoration. Some even harbor an elephant; but once you get into zoo operation you need a larger bankroll.

These animals should be displayed apart from the alligators, on a separate side of the bowl. You'll save money in the long run if you install well-built cages of concrete block, concrete floor, elevated off the ground so that the animal can be better seen and is not as vulnerable to colds. Chain link fencing is usually used as screen, the gage larger or smaller according to the animal's size.

Sanitation is a MUST for any well-run farm.

You'll see little alligators put to sleep this way, by turning them over on their backs—and it works equally well with big specimens such as this 12 footer. Trick is to get them to turn over. Some handlers say that rubbing their stomachs make no difference; pressure of blood on tiny alligator brain causes temporary blackout. Dangerous aspect: The alligator may "come to" at any moment. And he's usually angry about being manhandled!

Who hasn't been disgusted and repelled by the odor of a carelessly-operated zoo or animal display? This means daily cleaning and hosing down of cages and pens. It also means you'll need to be sure of a continuous supply of fresh water. Then too, dirty conditions can affect the animal's health.

You'll want to give your animals and customers protection from the elements. Florida's August sun can get mighty hot. Some roofed pens, and roofed walkways with gravel paths are good insurance against both sun and heavy summer rain. Again thinking of the customer, have you allowed him to sit down? Benches in a shady spot are welcome particularly by older visitors.

What about tours, lectures? There are two kinds of exhibits—the sort where you go in, wander around by your lonesome looking at unidentified alligators and animals, and wander out — and the kind where you're told a bit about the various specimens and a small demonstration is made during a 45-minute tour. The latter is by far the best way to give the customer his money's worth.

'Gator Farm Operation

Use plenty of identification signs — it helps and makes the animal more interesting. And offer tours as soon as you can. A well-informed talk and demonstration makes the visit doubly rewarding.

Your food bill for 'gators won't be high—but it will be steady. Here's how veteran operator C. C. McClung handles the problem at his LaPlace, Louisiana, Snake Farm. He has some 800 alligators, ranging from nine-inch size to 12-footers.

"I feed my captive alligators all they will eat twice a week through the summer and they do not eat through the winter months; they stop eating the first cold spell and start eating again in April. It costs me $50 a week to feed all my alligators. I am very conservative and buy 800 to 1,000 pounds of chicken heads from a large poultry company each week at five cents a pound delivered to me.

"I also raise crocodiles and caiman. I find that it is not necessary to vary the diet when feeding chicken heads as they get everything they need, especially calcium and lime which keep their teeth growing . . . If they were fed only red meat . . . after two or three years they would have no teeth.

"A large alligator eats less per pound body weight than small alligators. A 12-foot alligator will eat ten or 12 pounds once per week and no more. Where a three-foot 'gator will eat two pounds twice a week."

G. L. Stacey, of Musa Isle Seminole Indian Village, Miami, says 'gators are "relatively easy to keep."

Learning the ropes? You'd never guess it from this photo, but W. I. Drysdale (center) and his partner F. Charles Usina, (right) owned and operated — of all things — a haberdashery before buying the St. Augustine Alligator Farm! However, stranger things have happened. Another haberdasher became President. Most farm operators have had a lifelong interest in the outdoors, as have **Drysdale** and **Usina**.

'Gator Farm Operation

Most alligator farms feed their animals twice a week, but not at all during the winter months. Alligators in captivity, in Florida, do not hibernate in winter, but become more sluggish than usual.

Chunks of meat or fish, mainly fish, make up the usual bill of fare, which the alligator will take from the water, or on the ground of the pen.

Some operators advise that it is best to feed the animals always in the same way. If they become accustomed to having their food thrown in the water, they may overlook or refuse food left on the ground.

In captivity as in the wild, the alligator needs a varied diet. In addition to fish, they will accept cut meat, frogs, snakes, crawfish, snails. They need bone, and if bones are not readily available, should have bone meal sprinkled on their food.

They should not be fed salt meat or cured meat. Nor does the alligator relish decayed meat, which he will refuse. It is desirable, operators say, to add a little grass to their diet.

Newly captured specimens may refuse food for a while. Usually, they will accept food eventually if not disturbed or frightened too often. A small alligator may be force-fed by thrusting bits of meat down his gullet with a smooth wooden rod, but operators say this is seldom necessary.

If the alligators are kept in cold water, they will refuse food during the winter months; if the water is kept warm, they will eat throughout the year.

Operators say a 70-80 degree water temperature is best for alligators. This water temperature, not the air temperature, is the important thing. Like other reptiles, alligators should not be exposed to near-freezing temperatures, nor to high temperatures approaching 100 degrees. Water in which alligators are kept should not be allowed to become foul—it should be clean and fresh.

Advertising is a phase of the business not to be slighted. Highway billboards, postcards, newspaper and magazine advertisements are all basic. A comparatively new wrinkle is the use of radio and TV. Many farms get free plugs by allowing jungle-type programs on the nearest TV station to show a live specimen from the farm. The scientific-educational phase of the farms is important too.

Your farm will be of interest to writers doing newspaper and magazine articles, which is excellent publicity. It is possible that you may find your exhibit in the movies. Older Florida farms have been utilized as "props" and featured as short subjects for years by newsreels and in feature films.

In closing this discussion on the business, we can only cite a comment by veteran operator C. C. McClung: "I have never heard of an alligator farm going broke and closing up."

'Gator wrestling is a thing the tourist has heard about and wants to see. But you won't find it at too many farms. Why not? It is hard on a valuable animal; the alligator doesn't really want to wrestle anybody. It's dangerous and finally, it's an added expense. (Some wrestlers work for the collection they can take up.)

Granted this is true. But a first time visitor wants to see a man grab hold of a six-foot or bigger 'gator and push him around. You'll see this at St. Augustine Alligator Farm and Musa Isle in Miami. Other spots such as Allen's Reptile Institute and the Everglades Wonder Gardens offered a demonstrations with two or three-footers, putting them to sleep by turning them on their backs.

C. C. McClung, whose Snake Farm in LaPlace, Louisiana, is a big operation stocking some 800 or more animals, says he finds a major problem is keeping them from fighting: "When we get a mean one that fights all of the others, we have to separate it in a pen and wait until we make a sale." (This bears out comments by other handlers that alligators have personalities like other animals.)

He cautions about mud holes in pens with dirt floors: "When it rains, if there is the least bit of water standing in a low place, even an inch deep by twenty inches wide, they will wash it out larger and larger with their tails and legs—not digging, but just sloshing it out. I have seen them make a hole a foot deep and ten feet across in a month's time in rather hard ground. It seems they prefer muddy, rather than clear water.

"Wild alligators use this method when swamps begin to dry up. I have found alligator holes four feet deep and forty feet wide in the low coastal plains, with several large alligators in these holes."

You would probably be wise to have a veterinarian familiar with wild animals available. Although, in the case of the alligator, little doctoring is required: "The only time we have to treat an alligator," says McClung, "is when one has a foot or toe torn off by another 'gator. The alligator lives and the nub heals without treatment; it doesn't seem to bother or pain them when this happens. We have to watch the 'gators in the spring of the year for skin breaks when they fight. The teeth marks are sometimes deep and they will get screw worms in the wound if not treated with a screw worm preventative."

After near-extinction in some states, the alligator is finding that the law is more and more on his side.

Alligator Protection

IF ALLIGATORS COULD READ, they would probably be vastly encouraged by the following set of state laws regarding themselves. For from every indication, the alligator is not going to follow the buffalo into virtual oblivion. A number of the Southeastern states have realized the value of the homely saurian, and have taken measures to protect him. Things look bright for the toothy reptiles; the law is finally taking their side. The same cannot be said of the American crocodile, however. Although they enjoy protection as an endangered species, fewer than 500 of these beasts now inhabit the earth, with almost all of them located in South Florida. Wildlife experts are releasing crocodile hatchlings into Florida swamps in order to boost their population and thereby improve the species' chances of survival. One of the reasons that the American alligator, though numerous in many places, is carefully protected is because it is frequently confused with the endangered crocodile. The Endangered Species Act terms this "threatened due to a similarity of appearance (T/SA)."

FLORIDA

Florida state laws regarding alligators are extensive, covering the possession and sale of live 'gators, their skin, meat and eggs. Permits are required to kill alligators, and to possess or sell alligators or alligator products. Regulations govern all aspects of the operation of alligator farms. Farm operators must apply for a permit and file quarterly and annual reports with the state, disclosing their inventory of 'gators and eggs. Farms must also comply with state regulations regarding holding and rearing tank specifications, farm inspections, collection of eggs and hatchlings, etc. Farm operators must also apply for permits to collect alligator eggs. Nuisance alligators can only be trapped by persons bearing a special permit. Florida's efforts at protection have definitely been effective. Because alligators have become quite numerous in the state in recent years, Florida now holds an annual "alligator lottery". The state accepts applications for a 'gator hunting license, a drawing is held, and several hundred lucky folks receive a special permit to hunt or trap alligators during a short-lived open season. However, in order to participate in the hunt, they must first attend a state-run training course.

Alligator Protection

How the Indian alligator trap used in primitive Florida worked. Seeking food placed at the end of the S-shaped stakes, the alligator became firmly wedged in when he attempted to back out of the narrow space and his tail went between two of the stakes. Having no refrigerator, Indians would simply leave him there until food was needed.

SOUTH CAROLINA

All populations of the American alligator are protected in South Carolina. Alligator "control agents" are approved by the state Wildlife and Marine Resources Department; they are issued a permit and a tag for each and every alligator they take. They are allowed to keep the meat, but must turn over the hide to the state of South Carolina, which sells it and turns the net proceeds over to the control agent. Alligator meat may be sold, provided the seller is an authorized control agent or can prove that the meat was obtained legally from another state. Sellers of alligator products (hides, etc.) must obtain a state permit and make their records and places of business available for state inspection.

GEORGIA

The Georgia Department of Natural Resources administers a three-part alligator management program, including research and survey, alligator farming, and a nuisance alligator program. Every spring and summer since 1973, Georgia Game and Fish workers have participated in a night-time "alligator census". The alligators are counted at night because their glowing red eyes can easily be seen in the glare of a spotlight. Alligator nests are counted annually at Rhett's Island, in the Altamaha Wildlife Management Area, using a helicopter. This is done in order to gauge the success of alligator reproduction in the state. Georgia has fewer than ten alligator farms, which are regulated by state law and inspected by Georgia DNR. Alligators, eggs, and alligator products can be legally possessed only by those with special permits: licensed nuisance alligator trappers, alligator farms, zoos and other educational institutions. Alligators may be hunted only by state-licensed nuisance alligator trappers.

LOUISIANA

Louisiana allows alligator hunting, but severely restricts it. Alligators may be taken during daylight hours only, within the duration of the open season, and may not be taken from their nests or dens. Alligator hunters must purchase a hunting license, and also a "hide tag" for each 'gator they intend to take. Louisiana restricts the number of hunters by selecting them at a public drawing, as Florida does. Tags are issued for a specific geographic area and are non-transferable. Licenses are also required to sell meat or hide, to possess or exhibit live 'gators, to collect eggs or hatchlings, and to transport alligators or alligator products into or out of the state. Nuisance alligator hunters are selected by the state and must purchase a special permit.

NORTH CAROLINA

North Carolina has very few alligators, so they are especially protective of the ones they've got. It is unlawful to possess or sell alligator or alligator parts in the state, or to harm a wild alligator. Educational institutions such as zoos may possess them by special permit only.